INTRODUCTION TO THE PSALMS

Introduction
to the Psalms

CHRISTOPH F. BARTH

Translated by R. A. WILSON

§§§
§

CHARLES SCRIBNER'S SONS • *New York*

§§§

CONTENTS

§§§

INTRODUCTION TO THE PSALMS

§§§
§

§ 1. The Meaning of the Word 'Psalm'

From the linguistic point of view the word comes from the Greek *psalmos*, which in classical times meant no more than the music of a stringed instrument. Under the influence of the Greek Bible and of the advance of Christianity, however, it came to have the meaning 'song of praise', and the idea that such songs of praise might have been accompanied on stringed instruments gradually fell into the background or was completely forgotten.

The ancient Israelites, to whom—from the human point of view—we owe the origin of the Book of Psalms, appear to have had originally no term which applied to all the psalms. This book, of course, was put together from different sources, independent of each other, and only after this had taken place (cf. § 2), did it become necessary to find a title that would apply both to the whole book and to each individual poem. Other expressions familiar to readers of the Bible—e.g. 'judge', 'prophet', 'law' and 'sacrifice'—have a similar history: it was the systematizing of later generations which created these general expressions for groups of originally distinct phenomena.

Before such a generic name existed for the religious poetry gathered together in the Psalter, the Israelites used a number of different terms. Some of them can be taken to mean 'song with stringed instruments', 'song', 'prayer', 'poem' or 'song of praise' but it is no longer possible to discover their precise connotation—the poetic form referred to by each expression—and the particular occasion and manner of their performance.

After the whole collection had been gathered together, during the fourth and third centuries B.C., the term 'songs of praise' (*tehillim*) came into use. It is in fact far from appropriate to every one of the hundred and fifty psalms; one has only to consider the numerous lamentations which occur in the collection! In the Greek translation begun in the third century B.C., and which was to make the Old Testament much more widely accessible amongst Israel's neighbours, it was perhaps for this very reason that the expression chosen was not 'hymns' as might have been expected, but the apparently more neutral 'psalms'. Under the influence of the Hebrew *tehillim*, however, this Greek word soon took on the meaning 'songs of praise' which it has retained to the present day.

From the strictly literary point of view there is perhaps no single term that would be appropriate to *all* the psalms. The modern categories that might be applied (e.g. 'cultic lyric', 'religious songs' and 'prayers') are adequate only in individual cases and then only in a limited sense. Thus we shall have to retain the Greek expression 'psalms' with the Jewish interpretation 'songs of praise' that has been given to it. Seeing that the Chronicler in his history—not without justification in the older traditions of Israel—considers that the praise of God is the innermost substance of everything said and done in true worship of God, then perhaps the traditional term comes nearer to the truth after all.

§ 2. *The Origin of the Book of Psalms*

According to the popular conception David the king and musician had, under divine inspiration, composed the whole book. David was in fact involved in its earliest stages, and plays a notable part in many psalms (cf. § 20 below). But in its present form the Book of the Psalms is the result of a long development which was not completed until centuries *after* the time of David.

Anyone who seeks to understand this development should think of the way a *river* is formed: it takes innumerable little springs and streams to feed even the brook, and many brooks and small rivers must flow into its long meandering course before the full width of the river flows down to the sea! The present Book of Psalms took shape by a similar process. It began as single poems. After a few generations someone decided to gather together the legacy of the past, and to transmit to posterity the small book which was thus produced. The first collections of psalms of this sort may perhaps have come into being as early as the reign of David, or very shortly afterwards, that is, in the tenth century B.C.; three of them are still clearly recognizable today, viz., Pss. iii–xli, li–lxxii and cxxxviii–cxlv. Such collections were also produced under the later kings, although the guilds of musicians in the temple appear to have played an ever-increasing part in the composition; examples of these are the Psalms of the Sons of Korah (Pss. xlii–xlix, lxxxiv, lxxxv, lxxxvii, lxxxviii) and the Psalms of Asaph (Pss. l, lxxiii–lxxxiii); though of course they no longer exist in their original unified form. Even before the Exile an already extant collection must have been adapted in an 'elohistic' sense; cf. Pss. xlii–lxxxiii, in which the divine name Yahweh is replaced wherever possible by the more general term *elohim* (God). Pss. cxx–cxxxiv provide another example of a collection that was probably originally independent, although in fact their title 'songs of pilgrimage' is strictly applicable only to a few of them (e.g. Pss. cxxi/cxxii).

It was probably in the period after the Exile in Babylon that the collections that had been brought together up to that time were gathered into a single book, while at the same time material that belonged as yet to no collection, and was in part quite 'recent', was added, until the number of one hundred and fifty was completed. This was certainly the occasion when the psalms were put into their present order and arranged in five 'books': Pss. i–xli; xlii–lxxii; lxxiii–lxxxix; xc–cvi; cvii–cl. The editor's purpose in dividing the psalms into five parts can unfortunately no longer be ascertained. Perhaps it was done in order to assist in reading them in course in Jewish worship. And according to another very attractive explanation the editor intended the Psalter to appear as the five-fold answer of the congregation to the word of God—in the five books of Moses!

The Book of Psalms took at least six centuries to reach its present form. Kings, priests and prophets, but, above all, unknown poets and singers, constantly contributed their different gifts in this process. Of the Psalms more than of any other book of the Old Testament it must be said that *all* Israel, the people of God 'from generation to generation', took part in its composition.

§ 3. *The Number of Psalms in the Psalter*

This seems at first to be a superfluous question; the Hebrew text and all the ancient translations—with the exception of the Greek—reckon one hundred and fifty psalms. But a closer comparison shows that the content and length, the beginning and ending of particular psalms varied considerably as early as in pre-Christian times. So the number of psalms is not as fixed as is usually supposed.

1. Sometimes what in one tradition is regarded as two separate psalms is treated as a single psalm in another. Instead of the two psalms cxvi and cxlvii in Protestant translations of the Bible and in modern Hebrew editions, the translations of the Roman Catholic and the Orthodox Church give four, numbered cxiv–cxv and cxlvi–cxlvii. In other cases too, where at the present time only *one* psalm is counted as a unity, one has the impression that two originally independent psalms may have been joined together, cf. Pss. xix, xxii, xxvii, xl and cxliv, and for this reason they are often divided into halves (A and B).

2. On the other hand, two psalms are often given where another tradition presents only one. Thus Protestant translations give Pss. ix–x and cxiv–cxv each as two independent psalms, while other versions, following the ancient Greek

translation, recognise only one psalm (ix and cxiii) in each place. As far as Pss. ix–x are concerned, it appears in fact that it is right to number them as *one* psalm—just as Pss. xlii–xliii make better sense and are more easily understood if they are read as one (in spite of the fact that they are divided in all editions!).

3. We find the same psalm reckoned twice, in Pss. xiv and liii, the wording of which is virtually the same throughout, although they differ from each other in the divine name they use. Ps. lxx repeats—with the same alteration in the divine name—the final part of Ps. xl. Ps. cviii is compiled from the conclusions of Pss. lvii and lx, and is therefore not really a 'different' psalm at all; the psalm in 1 Chron. xvi was formed in a similar way (cf. § 13).

4. A few particularly short psalms, such as Pss. cxvii and cl, were probably not originally intended as separate psalms at all, but rather as the doxology or liturgical conclusion to the reading of the psalms, or as the conclusion of a shorter collection of psalms. A clear example of such a procedure is given by the last two verses of Ps. lxxii, which are unlikely to have belonged originally to this psalm.

All this makes it quite clear that the numbering given in our Bibles must be used with the greatest caution. One need not always be bound by this numbering in reading and understanding the psalms. In many cases it is necessary to make a very close examination to see what belongs together as a whole psalm and what does not, before one can go on to a detailed interpretation and explanation.

§ 4. The Headings of the Psalms

The majority of the psalms have a heading; amongst the exceptions are Pss. i, ii, xxxiii, xci, and cxix. Luther's German Bible, following the Hebrew text, gives altogether thirty-four psalms without a heading. But the ancient Greek translation had already found this state of affairs to be unsatisfactory and provided *all* the psalms—with the exception of Pss. i and ii—with headings.

When the verses were numbered in the sixteenth century of our era, these headings were regularly counted as the first verse or as part of it. This gives the impression to the reader of the psalms that the heading forms part of the main body of the psalm in question. In fact they are additions by a later hand—in most cases probably by the editor of the collection. These headings are the voice of the late Jewish community, though for the most part they are still pre-Christian. Although this to some degree limits their value, one still cannot pay too much attention to this most ancient 'commentary' on particular psalms.

We must distinguish between at least three types of psalm heading:

1. Notes on the literary form of a psalm and the right method of rendering it. To this category belong in the first place the general terms 'psalm', 'song', 'prayer', 'poem' etc., and in addition a large number of technical notes on the occasion and manner of their performance, the true meaning of which has unfortunately been lost. In Luther's Bible, and in other translations, these are rendered by phrases such as 'a song', 'on the Gittith' ('according to the Gittith'), 'on eight strings' and 'in the upper choir', but also 'a golden jewel', 'for the memorial offering', 'according to Lilies', 'according to The Beautiful Youth', 'according to Do Not Destroy', 'according to the Dove on Far-Off Terebinths' (Luther: 'according to the Voiceless Dove amongst the Strangers'), etc.—words which have become dear to many readers of the Bible, but which are only to be regarded as conjectures, and certainly not as translations. It is best to follow the modern translators, who simply reproduce the Hebrew expressions here without explanation, or refuse to make any attempt at all!

2. Secondly, the headings often contain the *names* of well-known biblical figures, who are supposed to have some special

connection with the psalm in question: David seventy-three times, Asaph twelve times, the Sons of Korah eleven times, Solomon twice, Heman, Ethan and the great Moses once each. From the earliest times these names have been regarded as indicating the author, but cf. § 5 below. Apart from this interpretation, it is possible to take them as referring to the person responsible for gathering together the smaller collections of psalms; 'of David' would then mean: 'one of David's psalms' that is, one of the collection of psalms compiled by David or on his orders.

3. The headings of Pss. xviii, li, lii, liv, lvi, lvii, lix, lx and lxiii contain exact details of the historical situation in which the particular psalm is supposed to have originated. As it is easy to see from the examples of Ps. li, such statements have no historical value; at least the conclusion of that psalm comes from the period after the destruction of Jerusalem and its Temple, and cannot therefore be considered also as a composition by David! These historical notes are better understood as a commentary of the Jewish community: the psalm reminds us of such and such a particular moment in the life of David (cf. § 20). In spite of all the mystery which today surrounds the headings of the psalms, they are not completely without significance. In that they constantly refer to the person of David, and reflect every possible form of intensive use of the psalms by the worshipping community, they perform an important service for the reader of the Bible.

§ 5. The Authors of the Psalms

Anyone who receives a letter, or takes up an article or a book, soon asks who is the sender or the author. We do not regard the name of the author as indispensable to the understanding of a writing, but as a very important clue. This interest in the identity of the author and in the circumstances of his life is one of the essential characteristics of western civilisation as it has grown up through the centuries. We are likewise very eager to learn who composed each individual psalm, and under what circumstances.

Unfortunately, in the form in which the psalms have been handed down to us, they give no clue to the identity of their authors. This is not simply due to the fact that the names of their authors have been accidentally lost or forgotten. Rather we must bear in mind that the psalms come from a cultural epoch and environment in which the modern interest in the personality of the author was still unknown. It is not without reason that with few exceptions all the other Old Testament writings have come down to us *without* the name of their author. Admittedly, at the time when the Holy Scriptures were being collected together and sifted (i.e., in the last four centuries B.C.) the practice was introduced of naming individual books after the principal persons who figured in them, and this led to the custom of ascribing all legal writings to Moses, all the psalms to David and all the books of Wisdom to Solomon; but this bears no relation to a serious interest in the name of the author in the modern scientific sense. The same is true of the names that occur in the headings of the psalms, so far as they purport to give information about the author.

In general the psalms can only be considered as 'literature' in a very limited sense. The historical works and prophetical books of the Old Testament may have been written, enlarged or edited in their present form by single or by several authors; whereas the psalms, in their great majority, originated in the worship of Israel. To ask who was the author would be as pointless as in the case of most folk songs, myths or sagas. It must sometimes have taken generations or centuries before a psalm was reduced to a fixed written form and so preserved for posterity.

In ancient Israel and early Judaism, men prayed and listened to the psalms without any knowledge of their authors, and we must try to imitate them in this. This may frequently mean that we have to give up any prospect of a detailed historical understanding, but it may perhaps make it possible for us to pay attention to the witness of the Israelite community and thus to 'the word' of scripture, instead of looking only for the utterances of particular personalities.

§ 6. *The Psalms as Poetry*

Anyone who knows the psalms only from Luther's Bible, the Authorized Version or the Prayer Book, or any such older translation, does not usually realise that he is reading poetry —that the psalms are in fact *poems* in the strict sense. We mean by *poetry* here a more exalted type of language distinguished from ordinary speech by certain formal and stylistic characteristics. It was not until the end of the eighteenth century that it was discovered that large parts of the Old Testament—the psalms among them—belong to this category. A comparison of the A.V. with the R.S.V. or any other modern translation which clearly demonstrates the poetic character of the psalms by the lay-out of the page at once casts a completely new light on the special nature and beauty of these texts.

But this discovery has been of great importance in another direction. If the psalms are poetry (and, moreover, Hebrew poetry, with their origin in the culture and civilisation of the ancient Near East), then they must be read and understood in accordance with the formal and stylistic patterns that regulate such poetry. The stylistic pathos, the accumulation of vivid images, the repetition of the same thought in many different forms, the apparently schematic structure that they often display, the absence of individual and personal traits— all this is easily understood, if the psalms are not prose, completely free in form, or even lyrics, but rather poetry of the type that developed in ancient Israel.

The discovery that the psalms are in poetic form, however,

is also important for the deeper understanding of their *content*. It is more and more recognised that the psalms are to be regarded as *sacral* poetry, so that they must be interpreted in the context of worship, and often actually provide examples of the liturgical language and practice of Israel, which is otherwise almost unknown to us. There are many passages in the psalms which have previously only been understood in a 'personal' sense, but which can be seen in a completely new light when they are related to a specific liturgical act (cf. §§ 16–18).

Special mention must be made here of some of the characteristic stylistic features of the psalms. The first is the 'parallelism' so familiar in Hebrew poetry, in which there is a very close similarity between each of two consecutive lines. Frequently the second line repeats in different words what has already been said in the first:

> 'O Lord, how many are my foes!
> Many are rising against me!' (Ps. iii. 1).

The second line, however, can also take up and develop further a thought begun in the first:

> 'For the Lord is a great God,
> And a great king above all Gods' (Ps. xcv. 3).

Sometimes the expression that conveys the main point is illuminated by an image which precedes it:

> 'As a hart longs for flowing streams,
> So longs my soul for thee, O God!' (Ps. xlii. 1).

Sometimes there occurs 'antithetic' parallelism, where the second line repeats the sense of the first in contrary terms:

> 'For the Lord knows the way of the righteous,
> But the way of the wicked will perish' (Ps. i. 6).

Secondly we should mention the very artificial device of the '*alphabetic*' psalm, which probably first came into use relatively late. These psalms have as many lines or verses as the

letters of the Hebrew alphabet, that is, twenty-two, and each
line or verse begins with these letters in order. This imposed
severe limitations on the poet's freedom, so that in fact the
result was often more artificial than artistic. The fact that
Pss. ix–x, xxv, xxxiv, xxxvii, cxi, cxii, cxix, and cxlv are
alphabetic poems is naturally not visible in the translation—
unless it be in the often surprising and seemingly arbitrary
way they flit from one subject to another.

Finally, a comment on the word 'Selah' interposed in
many places in the psalms (e.g. Ps. iii. 4, 8). Hitherto scholars
have come to no agreement as to what it means, but it seems
that it is either a musical or (more probably) a liturgical
sign.

§ 7. The Real Purpose of the Psalms

At first sight this seems to be another superfluous question.
Is it not obvious that in the worship of Israel the psalms
played the same part as the hymns and chorales of our own?
There is a good deal of truth in the title 'The Hymn-Book of
the Jewish Church' that has been given to the Psalter.

Later investigation has shown, however, that the psalms
were not used in this way until a comparatively late stage in
their development, and that the question of the original function of particular psalms casts a new and particularly illumi-
nating light on their meaning. The question of the name of
their authors, and the exact date at which they were composed, regarded in the past as of great importance for the
interpretation of the psalms, is now considered to be much
less important by comparison with the question of their
original purpose.

If the question is properly posed, many psalms begin to
reveal with astonishing clarity the occasion and the purpose
for which they were used in ancient times. And it also becomes obvious that by no means all the psalms were intended

for the worship of the Jewish community in the Temple or the synagogue. Some clearly have their place in the royal palace, others in the streets and gateways of the city or even in the open field; one can sense how very different the religious life of ancient Israel must have been from the restricted circumstances of the later Jewish community.

This means, then, that the psalms were intended for many quite different circumstances. There are liturgies for all kinds of regularly recurring festivals and even for isolated days of rejoicing, and for penitential gatherings which were convened in times of peril (drought, plague, war). Then there are prayers for individuals—especially numerous in the first half of the Psalter—the use of which can most easily be conceived of on the lines of Hannah's visit to the temple at Shiloh (1 Sam. i). Pilgrimages (Ps. cxxii), the entry into the sanctuary (Ps. c), sin-offerings and thank-offerings, confessions of sin, hand-washing ceremonies, the dedication of firstfruits, vows, departing blessings (Ps. cxxi) and many other cultic actions (Ps. cxxxiv) are echoed in one psalm or another or provide the context of whole psalms. There are many examples of religious poems that are meditative and didactic in content, or present a prophetic challenge, though it is admittedly often quite difficult to know to whom they were addressed and how they were used. This is much easier to see in the case of the many psalms in which the king is the central figure: there is hardly one important element of court ceremonial that is not covered.

The very numerous contexts in which the psalms were used often lead us to the limits of what would be called acts of worship according to modern ideas—and sometimes even beyond those limits. But there is no need for this in any way to hinder the rediscovery of the psalms. Perhaps the fresh and direct voice of the psalms is more rapidly perceived when their strangeness and antiquity has been recognised.

§ 8. Different Categories of Psalms

By 'formal category' (*Gattung*) modern biblical scholars—and indeed students of literature in general—mean a group of complete passages of poetry or prose which can be recognised as being associated by distinct characteristics of form, style and content. In the modern methods which appeared in the nineteenth century under the influence of J. G. Herder and W. M. L. de Wette and others, the importance of these formal categories for the understanding of literary documents, and therefore also of the psalms, was first recognised. In studying the psalms we have learned to pay very close attention to the characteristics of form and content in each individual psalm, not in order to interpret it as it were in isolation, or even by comparing it with a number of 'parallel' passages, but so that we can consider it strictly within the context, and in accordance with the purpose, of the group or category to which it belongs. Each particular psalm has now been designated as a hymn, a song of lament or thanksgiving, a wisdom psalm or a didactic psalm, etc., and can be understood and interpreted accordingly.

Although this was an important step forward, the allocation of the psalms to their different categories on the basis of purely *literary* characteristics soon proved unsatisfactory. Led by the famous scholar Hermann Gunkel, students of the psalms began to investigate the place of individual literary categories in the cultic or 'secular' life of Israel (*Sitz im Leben*) and to define their essential characteristics on this basis. At that time the many different ways in which the psalms could be used, of which we have already given a rough outline in § 7, were first elucidated.

The view always maintained by Gunkel, however, that all the psalms of ancient Israel were based on an essentially unchanged system of literary categories, gave way more and more to the realisation that as Israel's cultic life developed, these literary categories must also have undergone profound changes: we are dealing not only with many kinds of fragmentation, conflation and extension of existing forms, but also with their decay, and the appearance of new categories —even when they are clothed in the traditional dress of their predecessors.

Although scholars must always be grateful to Gunkel for his precise description of the most important literary categories and their cultic or, as the case may be, 'secular' background, they can no longer follow him in a too rigid application of his system, which sometimes sought and reconstructed categories where they were clearly lacking (cf. the excellent study by C. Westermann, *Das Loben Gottes in den Psalmen*, 1954; E.T. *The Praise of God in the Psalms*, by Keith R. Crim, 1965). Even the best and most complete system will fail to include a considerable number of psalms, which it is either impossible to fit into any category, or which can be included only by a forced interpretation.

Thus the reader of the psalms would do well to treat the distribution of the psalms into their appropriate literary categories in most recent commentaries—including the summary given below—as being no more than an attempted solution, and should investigate for himself the content and character of each particular psalm. The best way to begin this is to ascertain as far as possible who—besides God, who is always concerned—is the *person* who plays the decisive part in the psalm: the whole community gathered together, a clearly defined group within the community, an individual, or the bearer of a particular office, such as the king. Then the psalm should be examined to see whether its dominant note is one of lament and complaint or of praise and thanksgiving, or whether some other particular *purpose* can be perceived in it. If these two points can be decided with any certainty, it is usually possible to ascertain the occasion for which the psalm was originally used, and the way to a true interpretation is open.

§ 9. Psalms Intended for Individuals

In this and in the two following sections an attempt is made to survey the colourful profusion of literary categories in the psalms from one apparently quite external point of view, that of the person who is the main subject of the action described in the psalm.

Since they form by far the largest group in the Psalter, we begin with the individual psalms. The common denominator of the psalms we include in this group is in no way a relationship of content, literary form or cultic background but purely and simply the circumstance that they are chiefly concerned with individual members of the people of God: with the supplication and praise, with the happiness and sorrow, and in short with the life in the sight of God of each one of them. We say 'chiefly', because in Israel—by contrast with the psalm literature of the neighbouring nations, some of them much more ancient, cf. § 13—there is hardly a single psalm which is concerned only with an individual, and not also with the community in which he lives, the people of God.

1. We must first refer to the so-called *individual psalms of lament* (cf. Pss. iii–vii; xiii; xvii; xxii; xxv–xxviii; xxxv; xxxviii–xl; xlii–xliii; li; liv–lvii; lix; lxi; lxiii–lxiv; lxix–lxxi; lxxxvi; lxxxviii; cii; cix; cxx; cxxx; cxl–cxliii). Here the individual raises his voice in lamentation, imploring God to save him in his *time of trouble*. Sickness, misfortune, slander, hate, persecution, imprisonment, poverty or distress, and perhaps even several such trials have assailed him. The accumulation of different expressions of lamentation brought to a climax, which is a characteristic of the style of these psalms (cf. Ps. xxii!), makes it impossible to ascertain the nature of the suffering which the Psalmist 'originally' experienced and is now describing. Following an ancient cultic tradition, the psalm of lamentation is made up of the invo-

cation of the divine name, a request to God to hear and assist the worshipper, a lament, usually lengthy and exhaustive, an expression of trust in God's faithfulness or of certainty of being heard, a renewed call for help and a concluding vow, already leading even here to a song of praise. These prayers 'before God' have their natural place in the sanctuary; originally they must have been uttered there alone, while of course various kinds of cultic action were carried out at the same time. In many of these psalms of lamentation there are grounds for supposing that the worshipper was given an authoritative assurance that his prayer had been heard, by an 'oracle of salvation' from a priest, cf. 1 Samuel i. 17: 'Go in peace, and the God of Israel shall grant your petition which you have made to him.'

2. A complement to the psalms of lamentation and complaint are the very much less frequent individual *psalms of thanksgiving* (e.g. Pss. xviii, xxx, xxxiv, xl*a*, lii, lxvi*b*, cxvi and cxxxviii). In accordance with the meaning of the Hebrew *todah* they should be called songs of *praise*. Here the individual is offering praise to God for his salvation which has already taken place—from sickness, misfortune and despair. As in the case of the psalms of lamentation, the psalms of thanksgiving use a structure and formal language laid down by tradition, so that practically everywhere they consist of the following fixed parts: self-exhortation to praise, recalling of the distress that has been suffered, an account of the appeal for help, the answer and the deliverance, then the renewal of the vow and a paean of praise (often in very general terms). The aim of the songs is the exaltation of God by glorifying him in acknowledgement of his act of deliverance, so that even more clearly than the psalms of individual lamentation, their place is in the sanctuary in the presence of the assembled community; they would accompany sacrifices in praise of God (the so-called thank-offering). The example of Pss. cvii and cxviii shows that frequently several individuals discharged their vow in the same act of worship.

3. Amongst the individual lamentations there are quite a number to which this title is not strictly appropriate, because the lamentation passes straight on to a song of praise, sometimes quite early in the psalms, or towards the end as usual (cf. Pss. vi, xiii, xxii, xxviii, xxx, xxxi, xli, liv, lv, lvi, lxi, lxiii, lxiv, lxix, lxxi, lxxxvi, xciv, cii, and cxxx). It is equally unsatisfactory to explain this fact either by saying that separate psalms of lament and praise have been 'conflated', or by postulating a special 'intermediate' category. Strictly speaking, all psalms of individual lamentation contain expressions of trust and of certainty that they will be heard; thus they already contain all that leads to a song of praise. There was no such thing in Israel as lamentation for lamentation's sake, so that the 'individual psalms of praise' cannot be neatly separated from the psalms of lamentation. Lament and thanksgiving, petition and praise, are separated from each other like the two foci of an ellipse; somewhere between them, related to both, come various actual psalms. Thus the process of defining the situation underlying each psalm must be carried out with particular caution.

4. Some of the elements which regularly form part of the psalm of lamentation developed in the course of time into independent categories. The so-called *psalms of trust* should first be mentioned; they presumably arose from the passages expressing trust in the psalms of individual lamentation (cf. Pss. xi, xvi, xxiii, xxvii*a*, lxii, lxiii and cxxxi). In some psalms of lament the 'protestation of innocence' (cf. § 16) or a confession of sin is so prominent that one would tend to speak of actual *psalms of innocence* and *penitential psalms* (cf. Pss. vii, xv, xvii, xxvi and the well-known group of penitential psalms, vi, xxxii, xxxviii, li, cii, cxxx and cxliii). The so-called *vengeance psalms*, with which we find ourselves so little in sympathy—the best known example is Psalm cix—are best explained as an extension of the cry for help against the enemies of an individual, originating in the psalm of lamentation, cf. § 17. Finally the *oracle of salvation* originating in

the ritual of the psalm of lamentation occurs at least once (Psalm xcii) as an independent psalm.

5. A final group of individual psalms is characterised by the appearance of the individual simply as the *wise, pious* and *righteous* man. Sometimes he himself is the speaker, teaching, confessing his belief or meditating on it (cf. Pss. xix*b*, xxxvi, xxxvii, xlix, lviii, lxxiii, cxix, cxxxix; xiv=liii probably also belongs originally to this group); or else the community praises him as 'blessed' (cf. Pss. i, cxii, cxxvii, cxxviii, cxxxiii). It is exceptional for these *wisdom psalms* to be prayers in the usual sense of the word (e.g. Pss. xxxvi and cxix); in the first place they are spoken from one man to another, but—since they are words of faith—they can turn at any moment into prayers spoken to God (cf. lxxiii and cxxxix).

The *king* is also an individual in Israel. But we reserve the psalms in which he is the central person for special consideration (§ 11).

§ 10. *The Psalms of the Community*

Continuing our attempt at a summary division of the psalms into their formal categories, we come to those in which the principal personage is rather the people of God as a whole or—thinking in terms of the period after the exile— the Jewish *community*. The obvious external mark of the psalms of this group is the fact that normally a number of people are speaking (e.g., 'We shall praise Thee') or are spoken to (e.g., 'Give praise, O servants of the Lord'), but there are also psalms in which although apparently it is an individual, in fact it is 'Israel' who is speaking (Ps. cxxix). Since the individual psalms came very early to be prayed by the community—a fine example of this is Ps. cxxx—it is generally advisable not to divide these two groups too sharply from each other; in one the individual may be more prominent, in another the community.

1. Among the 'psalms' of the community there likewise appears to have been a series of categories identified by their form and content, but only a limited number remain recognisable. Amongst these there are first of all the so-called *lamentations of the people* (cf. Pss. xliv, lx, lxxiv, lxxix, lxxx, lxxxiii, lxxxv, while Ps. xc, ascribed to Moses, as well as Pss. xii, cxxiii, cxxv and cxxvi, also seem to belong to this category). Like the individual psalms of lamentation they consist of an invocation of God with an introductory petition, a lament, an expression of trust, a prayer for deliverance, and a vow; here also the last frequently leads to a hymn of praise to God, which sometimes even replaces it (cf. Ps. lxxxv). Characteristic of these lamentations is the appeal to God's faithfulness towards His chosen people; the distress of the present time (defeat, drought, famine, etc.) appears in sharp and terrible contrast to the background of the past. The most likely religious occasion for this kind of lamentation would seem to be spontaneously convened gatherings with fasting, sack-cloth and ashes.

2. A recognizable second category is formed by the psalms of *praise and thanksgiving* of the people—which probably once formed an exact parallel to the individual psalm of praise, cf. § 9. Single acts of God's intervention to deliver His people in the course of their history, e.g., the passage through the Red Sea or the raising of the siege of Jerusalem by Sennacherib, would originally at least have been the occasion for such songs of praise, uttered as a common prayer. Some idea of what such 'songs of thanksgiving for victory' looked like can be found from the example in Judges xvi. 23 ff.

> 'Into our hands God has given
> . . . our enemy,
> the ravager of our country,
> who has slain many of us.'

Surprisingly, only a small number of such psalms have been preserved in the Psalter, e.g., Pss. cxxiv, cxxix and lxvi, although the second half of the latter takes the form of an *individual* song of praise. Perhaps this category was replaced relatively early by other forms of hymn of praise.

3. Apart from the psalms we have already named as belonging to a particular category of community psalms, there is an even greater third group of about forty psalms, in which we are concerned with the community gathered together in the same way, and which cannot be allocated into proper 'categories'. For the 'categories' which are widely applied to this group—e.g., the 'hymns', the 'songs for Yahweh's coronation', the 'songs of Zion' or even the 'nature psalms'— are in reality not distinct categories at all. Almost *all* the psalms of this group have the characteristics of hymns; they are distinguished from one another not so much by the presence or absence of the praise of God, as by the particular *reason* for which he is praised. Sometimes the greatness of the *creator* (Pss. viii, xix, xxix, civ) is the principal subject, and sometimes the *sacred history of the nation* (Pss. lxxviii, lxxxi, cv, cvi, cxi, cxiv, cxxxv, cxxxvi); sometimes *Zion* (Pss. xlvi, xlviii, lxxvi, lxxxiv, lxxxvii, cxxii, cxxxvii) is the main theme, and sometimes the *kingdom of God* (Pss. xlvii, xciii, xcvi, xcvii, xcix and also Pss. xxiv, lxviii, lxxv, xcviii), while it is not unknown for two or several of these themes for the praise of God to be contained in one and the same psalm (e.g., Pss. xxxiii, ciii, cxiii, cxv, cxlv–cl). As opposed to the former custom of looking in each of these cases for distinct literary categories, it is better to suppose that the different themes of praise may have been connected with the original purpose and use of these psalms, and that we ought to consider them principally as *festival psalms* or *festival liturgies*. In this case not only historical events occurring only once, but regularly recurring festivals would have given rise to this kind of community psalm.

If this view is correct, we must inevitably ask for which particular feast a particular psalm was intended. Pss. lxv, lxvii and cxlv could be connected with the *harvest* festival and Ps. cxiv perhaps with the feast of the *Passover*, but it is not possible to establish a convincing or even probable connection between any given psalms other than these (such as Ps. lxxxii) and the great festivals of Israel as they are known to us from the Pentateuch. Did these festivals take on a different meaning in the course of time, or were perhaps other feasts celebrated besides these, or even in their place—feasts which in the festival calendar of the Pentateuch (Exod. xxiii and xxxiv; Lev. xxiii; Num. xxvii–xxviii; Deut. xvi) are either not yet mentioned or had already dropped out of use?

In the last forty years scholars have made an intensive study of the first of these two possibilities and have established that the autumn 'feast of the wine-harvest' in particular underwent a violent change in its significance. As the name suggests, it was a feast of rejoicing, an agricultural feast, and in consequence very close to the nature religion of Canaan (see Judges xxi. 19). The older pattern of its celebration was augmented, probably very early, by the originally nomadic custom of dwelling in booths (Deut. xvi. 13–15). The genuinely Israelite form of the feast, based on the nation's sacred history and now in fact called the feast of the *Tabernacles*, seems only to have prevailed gradually (Lev. xxiii. 42 ff.): it was celebrated at the common sanctuary of the confederation of tribes, and it was the practice—along the lines of Deut. xxvii and Josh. viii—solemnly to renew the covenant with Yahweh, the God of Israel (as perhaps in 1 Sam. 1, 3, 21, 24; Hosea ix. 5; Pss. l; lxxxi; xcv). It was certainly also celebrated in Jerusalem during the time of the kings as the feast of the covenant, except that there the covenant of Yahweh with David and the choosing of Zion as the place for the sacred Ark (cf. 2 Sam. vi) was the central theme of what took place. In post-exilic times this ancient feast of Tabernacles was restored (Neh. viii. 17), although it was probably soon amalgamated with *New Year's Day*, which occurred at almost the same time, while in addition a new dimension was given to its content in the prophetic celebration, as a fact, of the *enthronement* and everlasting *kingdom of Yahweh*.

It is clear that the more accurate picture of the feast of the wine-harvest or Tabernacles that is now available, although it is still to a considerable extent hypothetical, casts a surprising light on the background of very many of the festival hymns in the Psalter. With the 'discovery' of a previously unknown aspect of the feast of Tabernacles, there was admittedly always a tendency to relate as many as possible, or indeed practically all of the festival psalms to this single aspect, and even to try to include a number of psalms outside this group. Such wide generalizations usually prove untenable on closer examination. The 'Feast of the enthronement of Yahweh', which a few years ago was regarded as of primary importance for the Psalter, is now applied within much narrower limits; the same is no doubt to be expected for the 'feast of the renewal of the covenant', which today is frequently regarded as the principal cultic background of the festival psalms, and even more in the case of the cultic and mythical interpretation, which purports to see in every second psalm a ritual of the New Year festival on the Babylonian pattern.

If as a result of the elucidation of the Israelite festival calendar we are in a position to draw a more concrete picture of the background of many of the community psalms—even though this cannot always be done with certainty—that would be in itself a sufficient gain.

§ 11. The Royal Psalms

For many readers perhaps this title brings to mind David, the king and musician, whose name occurs in the heading of no less than seventy-three psalms (cf. §§ 4 and 20). But by 'royal psalms' Old Testament scholars are simply referring to those of the psalms in which the important figure in the text is the king—some king of Israel or Judah. Psalms ii, xviii, xx, xxi, xlv, lxxii, lxxxix, ci, cx, cxxxii and cxliv are usually included in this group. Psalm xlv is probably the only one that originated in the northern kingdom.

Israel certainly did not possess royal psalms until the time of the kings, that is till the reign of Saul or David at the earliest. One might suppose that with the fall of the kingdoms of Israel (722 B.C.) and Judah (587 B.C.) this type of psalm would also be doomed to disappear. In fact they survived the kingdoms, and retained their significance for Israel and for us. This is only partly explained by the fact that the royal psalms were no longer taken as referring to earthly kings, but were understood as prophecies of the Messiah, the king who should come at the end of time, with the result that they always had a contemporary relevance. The primary reason for their survival lies in the *nature* of the kingdom they described.

The Israelite kingdoms were in many respects similar to those of their neighbours in Palestine and Syria, not least in the brief zenith of their power and rapid decline; but they had their own special features. The most ancient tradition of Israel represents the basis of the kingdom as a series of historical events—not, as in other nations, as a timeless and eternal natural order embracing heaven and earth. In the picture this tradition portrays, especially in the books of Samuel and Kings, this kingdom is rooted in what had been begun centuries earlier, and had been constantly renewed ever since, the choosing, gathering together and separation of Israel as the property, first-born child, people and worshipping community of their God. The decisive feature in the nature of their kingdom was not a natural ideal of royal authority, but the choosing of Israel. It stood or fell by the degree to which it was the historical expression of this reality. There was a time when it satisfied this demand, and after that, at a given moment, it came to its historical end. But if the reality of the kingdom was the choosing of Israel, and if this reality was miraculously continued even *beyond* the period of the kings, then the kingdom itself was able and was bound to remain a present reality. This presumably also explains why the royal psalms have maintained their place in the worship of the Jewish community at all periods.

From the external point of view, the royal psalms are comparable to the *court poetry* which was so highly developed in the ancient East. The background consists of court ceremonies pure and simple: the anointing or coronation of a new king (Pss. ii and cx)—perhaps also their recurrent anniversaries (as perhaps Pss. xxi and lxxii)—the wedding of the king (Ps. xlv), the king's setting out to war (Pss. xx and cxliv) or the celebration of victory (Ps. xviii, cf. Ps. xx. 5). Ps. cxxxii suggests the celebration of a feast in the royal temple, and the well-known lines in Isaiah ix. 5–6 ('Unto us a child is born') would lead us to suppose that even the birth of a prince was the object of a solemn celebration at court. Sometimes the speaker is the king (e.g. Ps. ci), sometimes the people (Ps. xxi) or someone on their behalf (Ps. cx); on occasion a priest or prophet speaks in the name of God, or else different voices follow one another in ceremonial fashion (Pss. ii and cxxxii).

A feature of all court poetry, including that of the Israelites, is a tendency to the exaltation of earthly reality, and especially to the idealization of the figure of the king: not only his subjects but all the nations of the world expect to profit from his just rule (cf. Pss. ii and lxxii); in the same way the 'religious' imagery underlying and adorning it can safely be taken as a feature of courtly ceremonial at every period and in all countries. It would be foolish to reject the genuinely 'secular' characteristics of the royal psalms in the Bible, and to reserve these poems from the very beginning for a 'spiritual' interpretation.

But at the same time as we recognise their secular nature, we must also emphasise the distinctive character of the psalms; as we have already argued, it is to be found in the distinctive characteristics of the kingdom in Israel and Judah, notably in the linking of the idea of the kingdom with the ancient tradition, surviving in constantly renewed forms, of the choosing of Israel. We do not deny that the royal psalms in the Bible are concerned with the fortune and misfortune of each particular king and of the population of his kingdom; but they are concerned at the same time with the 'anointing of Yahweh', with the 'people of Yahweh' and with the individual 'worshippers' of which the nation was made up. Is this simply a 'religious' veneer and elaboration added to the fundamentally 'secular' subject of these psalms? If the tradition of the choosing of Israel had first appeared in the period of the kings, this view would be correct. In reality, however, it was anterior to the kingdom both in time and in its whole conception, so that it is that tradition which is the primary origin of the royal psalms, while the court poetry of the ancient Near East provides only a secondary basis for their understanding and interpretation. This can be clearly seen from two facts.

In the first place it is notable that many *royal* psalms, from the point of view of form and content, belong to the category of *individual psalms*. The prayer which the king utters when he is oppressed by his enemies, in its formal pattern belongs to the 'psalms of lamentation', while the king's song of thanksgiving after a hard-won victory is in form and content an 'individual psalm of thanksgiving'. But an opposite effect is also visible, the strong influence of the royal psalms on the individual psalms of lamentation and thanksgiving: that the latter can quite easily refer to a wide circle of kings (Ps. cxxxviii. 4) and nations (Ps. xxii. 28 ff.), and employ military images, is most easily explained in this way. Which side gave and which received the most can scarcely be decided now; the process of 'democratization' of court poetry, a clearly discernible process in the literature of the ancient Near East, must have been preceded or accompanied in Israel by a similar process in the opposite direction. At least we can conclude from the close relationship between these two groups of psalms that according to the outlook that underlies them, the king and the individual in Israel *belong together*. But this means that in the prayers of an individual the king is always more or less closely associated with him, while in the prayers of the king the individual Israelite is included at the same time (cf. Pss. lxi. 7; lxiii. 11; 1 Sam. ii. 10 with Ps. xxii and likewise with many other individual lamentations and songs of thanksgiving, which perhaps were originally prayers of the king).

Secondly, however, the close connection between the royal psalms and the large group of psalms of the people, or of the community, must be emphasized. If the king regarded himself as the 'anointed of Yahweh' and if this title marked him as the chosen representative of the chosen people, then his own prayer was almost bound to be also a prayer in the name of, and in union with, the chosen people (cf. Ps. lxxxix), while on the other hand at solemn gatherings the people would regard the king as their own representative (Ps. lxxxiv). The example of Ps. xxviii (vv. 7–9) shows in the most striking way how closely the affairs of the individual, the king and the people were connected.

We must conclude with a short comment on the *messianic psalms*. It is widely held that the witness to the Messiah who was to come is manifestly clear in the royal psalms—and in particular Pss. ii, xlv, lxxii, lxxxix, cx, cxxxii—because they do not speak so much of the historical kings as of a prince who is to bring salvation at the end of time, that is, of the 'Messiah'. This separate treatment of certain psalms, however, is unacceptable, because it involves the denial or neglect of their original historical significance. It is true that the royal psalms were read and interpreted in a 'messianic' sense by the Jewish community—and even more by the early Church. But the same is also true of the other psalms almost without exception (cf. § 21). It is advisable, therefore, to give up the distinction between 'messianic' and 'non-messianic' psalms altogether and instead to examine *every* psalm to see whether and to what degree it actually proclaims a future Messiah.

§ 12. Psalms Outside the Psalter

With the discovery of the poetic treasures of the Bible (cf. § 6) attention was directed at once to the psalms, and poems similar to psalms, which are found in considerable numbers here and there in the other books of the Old Testament. The best known are the 'Song of Moses' (Deut: xxxii. 1–43), the 'psalm of Hannah' (1 Sam. ii. 1–10), the 'psalm of Hezekiah' (Isa. xxxviii. 10–20) and the 'psalm of Jonah' (Jonah ii. 3– 10); the three last poems belong to the category of individual psalms, whereas the first is rather a psalm of the community. It is easy to see that the 'Song of Israel at the Red Sea' (Exod. xv. 1–18) and the 'psalm of Habakkuk' (Hab. iii. 2–19) are psalms of the people or of the community. In the 'Lamentations' which in our Bibles are usually placed after the Book of Jeremiah, a complete small collection of psalms is preserved; the speaker in them is frequently an individual—especially in the third of these psalms, the beginning of which gives the impression of being an individual psalm of lamentation— but in view of the object of their lamentation, the fall of Zion, they should probably be regarded as psalms of the commu- nity. Although these 'Lamentations' were only connected relatively late with the prophet Jeremiah, there is on the other hand a series of psalms or fragments of psalms, which belong to the book of Jeremiah proper, and may very prob- ably go back to the prophet himself (e.g., Jer. xv. 15–18; xvii. 14–18; xviii. 19–23). Since in most Bibles they are not recognisable from the layout as poetry, these 'individual lamentations of Jeremiah' are still unknown to many readers. For the psalms of the *New Testament* see below, § 22.

Different explanations are possible why these 'psalms out- side the Psalter' have not been gathered into the book in which they rightly belong: *either* at the time when the Book of Psalms was compiled they already had a fixed place as part of an 'older' book, *or* else they were not composed until later, and for that reason could not be accepted into the Psalter. In both cases it must not be forgotten that we are dealing with genuine psalms, which in theory could just as well be included in the Psalter. The proof of this is provided by the royal psalm of praise, which has found a place both in the Psalter (Ps. xviii) and within the second book of Samuel (2 Sam. xxii).

Scholars attach great importance to these scattered psalms. In the first place the increase in the material for use in comparison makes possible a more accurate picture of the different stylistic types, and their development, especially at a later period. But more than anything else, the religious poetry that has not been taken into the Psalter provides an invaluable insight into the function of the psalms in the religious life of Israel; the narrative context in which, say, the 'Song of Israel at the Red Sea' or the 'psalm of Hannah' are set shows the actual situation to which—in the view of the biblical narrator—these psalms belong. We learn something from this about the way in which the Jewish community related to particular human situations the psalms that had come down to them from the past. This was often done in a very free fashion, with little regard to the original place and meaning of the psalms they used—cf. e.g., 1 Sam. ii and Jonah ii with their present context—but in other cases we are given authentic information concerning their original use: since the story of the escape from Egypt, Exod. i ff., is recognised in the most recent studies as taking the form of a liturgical reading for the feast of the Passover, the 'Song of Israel at the Red Sea', Exod. xv, now included within it, can be regarded with reasonable certainty as a true Passover psalm, and this increases the probability that Ps. cxiv can be regarded in the same way. There is also much to be learned from the fact that the compiler of Isa. i–xxxix takes it for granted that when he adds a series of stories concerning Isaiah from the second Book of Kings he can put a psalm (Isa. xxxviii. 10–20) in the mouth of King Hezekiah: either he regards it as a genuine royal psalm, or he holds the view that what was originally an 'individual psalm of lamentation and thanksgiving' can be used without further ado as a royal psalm!

All this should make quite clear why we must pay constant attention to this 'diaspora' of psalms in our reading and interpretation of the Psalter.

§ 13. Psalms Outside the Bible

It is not only in the Bible that psalms are to be found; world literature contains religious poems, hymns and prayers which in form and content can safely be compared with the biblical psalms and with some reservation can themselves be called 'psalms'. In the same way, other literary forms in the Bible have their parallels elsewhere in world literature: one has only to think of the stories of the beginning of the world, and of the origin of sanctuaries, of the law books and the historical works. To make a comparison between the Bible and these parallels makes us even more conscious of the unique and unparalleled features of its message.

As far as the psalms outside the Bible are concerned, we must content ourselves in the present work with a reference to those which have a direct relationship to the composition of the biblical psalms. Such a connection exists, above all, where there has been an influence in one direction or another between the psalms within and those outside the Bible, that is, where the relationship between the two groups is such that one is the original pattern or an imitation of the other. In the first case, we find *prototypes* of the psalms in the ancient Near East, while in the second case we are discussing *Jewish imitations* of the biblical psalms.

For many readers the suggestion of 'prototypes' of the biblical psalms will be a surprising one. But how can one avoid the use of this concept, in view of the tradition of religious poetry, more than two thousand years old, amongst the people in

whose midst Israel came into being, and who were the school
in which they learned so much of their own culture? The
poets who wrote the biblical psalms knew this tradition and
learned from it; only against this background—and also of
course in conflict with it—could a peculiarly Israelite tradition have arisen.

We owe our knowledge of the ancient Near Eastern prototypes of the psalms to the literary documents which since the
nineteenth century have been brought to light by the spade of
the archaeologist: in the Nile valley and in Mesopotamia,
but also in Palestine, Syria and Asia Minor. For the most
part it has only become possible to read and understand them
in the present century, that is, since the deciphering of
Egyptian, Sumerian, Accadian and many other long-for-
gotten languages of the ancient Near East. No later than
1500 B.C. there existed in *Egypt* hymns and royal psalms of
victory and thanksgiving, which show a high degree of
stylistic feeling; that they were known to those who composed
the Israelite psalms is shown by a comparison of Egyptian
hymns to the sun-god with Ps. civ, which in some passages is
strikingly reminiscent of them. Of even greater importance
was the literary legacy of *Mesopotamia*; its main outlines
had already taken shape as early as the fourth millenium B.C.
in the hands of the Sumerians; it was taken over and enlarged by the Babylonians, and collected and preserved for
posterity by the zeal of Assyrian kings. It contained many
types of prayers and hymns to gods, mostly intended for the
king, but especially of numerous psalms of lamentation and
penitence, which exercised a decisive influence on the development of this category in the Psalter, where there are
also many examples of such psalms.

How did these 'prototypes' come to be known in Israel?
Probably only a very small fraction of them were known
directly. There are many reasons for supposing that Egyptian
and Babylonian influence reached the Israelites by way of
smaller nations and civilisations which in their own turn had

been influenced by them. It is known today that both the earlier inhabitants of *Canaan* and their northern neighbours the *Phoenicians* had their own psalm literature, and the same can also be presumed of other nations in the region of Syria and Palestine, although at the moment we possess no examples.

What then was the nature of the influence exercised by these foreign prototypes on the psalms of the Bible? It is usual to distinguish here between an influence on the more external, *formal* aspects of the psalms, and an influence on their *content*, and there is a tendency to regard the influence on the biblical psalms as a purely formal one. In reality the Israelites adopted from their predecessors, together with the literary categories and the language appropriate to each category, essential elements which decisively affected the content of their psalms. One such element was certainly the 'praise of the supreme God, the creator of heaven and earth', with which, according to the very ancient tradition of Genesis xiv, Abraham became acquainted from Melchizedek the king of Salem. Another element was the description of the marvels of nature, which we find for example in Pss. viii, xix*a*, xxix and civ; there are good reasons for supposing that Ps. xxix is an Israelite 'adaptation' of a hymn to the Canaanite storm-god Hadad. But even the hymns that enumerate the praises of God, the prayer of the king in the name of his people, the lamentation with its repeated 'why?' and 'how long?' or the vow and the thanksgiving at the end of so many psalms, are material adopted from outside, the significance of which it is not possible to describe as purely 'formal'.

On the other hand, it must not be forgotten that there were limits to the influence on the biblical psalms of their ancient Near Eastern prototypes. Israel learned, borrowed and imitated, and yet, astonishing as it may seem, never ceased to be Israel. The psalms of the Bible are addressed to Yahweh, the God of Israel, and not to some divinity or number of gods. In the midst of the Near Eastern world, which worshipped

in a divinity the personification of the social and cosmic
order, this means that Israel acknowledged a God who was
above that order, bringing his saving work to perfection in
history. This faith explains the distinctive nature of the biblical psalms: their freedom from any wheedling or magical
attempt to gain the grace of heaven, their steadfast insistence
on basing everything on the fact of the covenant and the
choosing of Israel, with their understanding of the proper relationship between the glory of the creator and the glory of
the redeemer, their 'demythologised' human language about
the king, and much else that could be mentioned here. There
is no danger of any confusion between the psalms of the Bible
and the examples that they follow!

In this respect the relation between the biblical psalms and
their *Jewish imitations* is less simple; they were composed in
the same tradition, for the most part in the same language
and in constant dependence on the biblical psalms, so that the
difference between the two can only be appreciated on a very
close examination. For example, anyone reading the five
apocryphal psalms of David, preserved in Syriac and partly
in Hebrew, could actually suppose that he was looking at
'genuine' biblical psalms. The same is true—to a more or less
marked degree—of the 'thanksgiving of Sirach' (Ecclus. li. 1–
12), of the penitential 'prayer of Manasseh' (an apocryphal
addition to 2 Chron. xxxiii), of the so-called 'song of the
Three Children' and of the 'prayer of Azariah' (an addition
to Dan. iii. 23), as also of the eighteen 'psalms of Solomon'.

The reason why these psalms are not included in the
canonical books of the Bible is in the first place the quite
simple fact that most of them were not composed until the
last two centuries B.C., that is, after the Bible had been
brought to its present form, or at the very end of that period.
But there are other material reasons. Although outwardly
they imitate the biblical forms faithfully, the quite different
spirit in which they were composed is frequently noticeable.
They are no longer concerned with Israel, in the sense in

which the prophets understood the term, but principally with the interests and ideas of a Judaism that had become a 'religious community', or even with those of particular late Jewish groups and sects. The biblical psalms must be used as a corrective in grasping and evaluating what is genuine and true in these imitations.

This judgement is reinforced by the psalms discovered in the caves near Qumran since 1947. There is first a long hymn attached to the 'Manual of Discipline'. It takes the form of an elaborate *promise* to praise and obey God for ever, concluding with a *blessing* of God for taking the Psalmist out of the lot of sinful mankind, 'opening the heart of thy servant unto knowledge', and taking him into the holy community. Its place and content have caused many scholars to consider that it was used by newly-initiated members of the Qumran community.

The collection of 'Hymns of Thanksgiving' presumably used in the community's daily worship falls into two groups: those beginning 'I give thee thanks, O Lord', and those beginning 'Blessed art thou, O Lord'—both reflecting clearly defined forms of liturgical composition in the early synagogue. Both these songs of praise and the 'Hymn of the Initiants' reflect the style and language of the canonical psalms—there are the wicked enemies, the parallelism, etc. —but also reproduce the technical language and ideas of the distinctive theology of the community. This is an extreme case of the adaptation of the traditional psalmody to the needs and ideas of an exclusive and sectarian Judaism.

§ 14. The Hebrew Text and its Translations

Having discussed the literary affiliations of the Psalter, we can now concentrate our attention on the proper object of this introduction. As an essential premiss for the correct understanding of the Psalter, we must first examine the question of the *exact words* of these psalms. For who can properly understand a text without making sure first that he has the correct reading in front of him?

But the task of establishing the correct, that is, the 'original' wording is not an easy one. Neither the A.V., the R.S.V., nor any other translation—however thorough it may be—is able to present it; for every translation, as the word implies, has resulted from a 'transference' of the original Hebrew words; that is, their transference into the language and thought-forms of a community of men separated from the author by thousands of miles and thousands of years. In spite of every attempt at scientific accuracy, the insinuation of all kinds of new shades of meaning, foreign to the sense of the original words, or even opposed to it, is inevitable. Modern study has removed numerous misinterpretations and has made possible translations of an accuracy hitherto unknown, but it is the best scholars who are most aware of the limits of their work. Thus every new translation must be content with making a very slight advance over its predecessors.

One of the greatest hindrances to the production of a really trustworthy translation is the fact that the original text—the 'Hebrew truth' as St. Jerome called it—no longer exists in an uncorrupted form. What is accepted at the present time as the basic Hebrew text, and is regarded by many as the original wording, may perhaps be close to the original, but can in no way be equated with it. It has passed through too many hands and has been considered, interpreted, and reshaped by too many minds, for it still to be regarded now as the 'original' text. To understand this, it is sufficient to consider the *vowel signs* which Jewish scholars added to the text, which previously had no indication of vowels, quite late in the Christian era; this they did on the basis of a sound knowledge of the Hebrew language, but *also* on the basis of a particular interpretation of the written word which was not necessarily or invariably in accord with the original text. Or one might consider the innumerable possibilities of *scribal error* which could have occurred as the text was recopied century after century, and in fact did occur: they are mostly insignificant, scarcely altering the meaning of the words, but sometimes they are so far-reaching that single words or whole phrases and verses have been garbled, altered, or rendered totally incomprehensible. The same is true of the text of the Old Testament as a whole, but is particularly evident in the Psalter, where a few variations which took place as early as the pre-Christian period can be seen in the psalms that are preserved in a double tradition (cf. § 3).

Thus we have to reckon with the fact that many psalms— including the most beautiful and the best-known—have come down to us in a corrupt text. Examples of these 'corruptions' are Pss. ii. 11–12; viii. 1–2; xviii. 12–13; xxii. 29; xxiv. 5; lxxiii. 24–26; lxxxiv. 10; xc. 10; cx. 3, 6–7; cxli. 5–7. Naturally such passages present considerable difficulty to the translator; it is hardly surprising that in every case numerous different solutions have been put forward. The very oldest translations (the Greek, Aramaic, Syriac and Latin) frequently differ from one another, and this is even more true of more recent translations, right up to the most modern versions, such as are given in scholarly and popular commentaries on the scriptures. Translations made by individual scholars on their own responsibility show greater freedom in their attempts to solve the difficulties than the editions of the Bible officially prepared by Church authorities. Although the greatest caution should be shown in accepting these freer versions, it must be remembered on the other hand that a slavish reliance on the Hebrew text throughout does not always lead to a reproduction of the original wording and meaning. Nevertheless, there is sufficient reason to be thankful that on the whole the psalms have been handed down to us so little damaged, and with their meaning so little obscured.

§ *15. The Right Way to Pray*

The Psalter has more than once been called 'the *Prayer Book* of the Bible'. In so far as it suggests that the Psalter consists of nothing but prayers, this title is not strictly accurate—unless one gives so wide a meaning to the concept of prayer that it can in fact be used of all the material in the Psalter. But this would be to ignore the not inconsiderable number of psalms which are in fact addressed to men and not to God (Pss. i, ii, xxxii, xlv, etc.). So the Psalter must be spoken of as a 'prayer book' with some caution, and with due regard to the limits within which the term is applicable.

A much happier title for the Psalter would be that of a '*school* of prayer', that is, a book from which one can learn what prayer means, and 'how to pray in the right way'. For *all* the psalms have something to teach us in this direction—even those which from their form and content cannot be called prayers in the true sense. For they all belong to the complex of words and acts of worship which is also the natural place of prayer.

But what is the 'right' way to pray? A rich variety of possible variations in the form and content of a prayer has been gathered together from all over the world, from every nation and from every century, by students of comparative religion. It is not easy to answer this question with a reasonable generalisation which at the same time accurately and fully defines the true meaning of prayer. In the very finest and clearest definition of the 'true' prayer there is constantly a risk of simply reproducing a personal opinion. We will limit ourselves, therefore, to describing the most important features of true prayer, as they are displayed in the psalms themselves, and can confidently leave the decision as to whether the psalms in fact describe 'the right way' to pray to their own intrinsic power of conviction.

1. To pray in the right way means in the psalms to speak to God in a way that corresponds to His own words to men. What *men* say to God—for this is what takes place in prayer —can only be an answer to the words of *God* which came first and made it possible. When the Psalmists pray, they base their prayers on what God has spoken to His people: what they say to Him goes back to his own words. Naturally the Psalter contains spontaneous appeals, lamentations, supplications and vows, just as it contains spontaneous praise, glorification, rejoicing and thanksgiving. But all these utterances are made not in indeterminate circumstances or with any and every kind of religious presupposition, but are consciously set within the 'sphere of activity' defined by the name, word and acts of the God of Israel. Only within this sphere, that is, in recognition and acknowledgement of this word and these acts, and in unswerving adherence to them, can one pray 'in the right way' according to the psalms.

2. This means that it is also essential to true prayer that in its content, nature and purpose, it must always be basically and fundamentally *praise of God*. In the 'songs of lamentation' which are so frequent in the Psalter this is not of course so fully expressed; in Ps. lxxxviii, scarcely a glimmer of hope— far less of praise and thanksgiving—breaks through the darkness. And yet there is a deep significance in the fact that the Psalter as a whole is called by the Jews *tehillim* ('songs of praise', cf. § 1). It is quite obvious that the *aim* of every group and category of psalms is the increase of the praise of God: some by seeking and opening the way towards praise, through lamentation, supplication and a vow, or through meditation and instruction, and others by expressing this praise themselves. Based as they are on the words of God to his people, the psalms are bound to present the view that man's salvation is to be found in giving the due answer to those words; but this answer is given when men take part in the praise of God. A metrical paraphrase of Ps. c makes this point very forcibly: 'to *praise* the Lord is our task'.

3. A further sign of true prayer is the *humility* that is by
nature proper to every human attempt to speak to God. True
prayer comes 'out of the depths'—in Luther's paraphrase:
'out of deep distress'. It is no accident that the Psalter contains so many lamentations and touching descriptions of
human guilt and human misery; one might be inclined to
think that the whole book bore witness to a pessimistic outlook on life. But this appearance is false; all the Psalmists
are concerned not with distress as such, but with taking it
before God, who they know is the judge and at the same time
the redeemer, with sovereign power over all distress. Thus
they seek a way out of the abyss of misery and up to the
heights, to the 'broad place' where they belong, according to
the revealed will of God. But the Psalmists contend that these
heights are only reached when man, the mighty, the rich and
the strong, as he regards himself, abandons his pretensions in
the sight of God, so that he now comes before Him only as
one who is poor and wretched, and in need of redemption.
This lowliness, which would otherwise signify for him nothing
but derision and rejection, he now experiences as the beginning, and even as the goal and the innermost mystery of his
exaltation (cf. Ps. lxix. 29: 'Let thy salvation, O God, set me
on high').

4. All the characteristics that we have so far mentioned can
be summed up by saying that true prayer, as the psalms
understand it, must be uttered in union and solidarity with
Israel—the people of God—and sometimes even with foreign
nations. The large number of 'individual' psalms in the
Psalter seems to contradict this; it is not the whole community speaking here with one voice, but an individual, and often,
in fact, someone rejected by God and men. But one must not
be misled by the term 'individual'. The formal and traditional language, the way the community is regularly drawn
into the suffering and praise of the individual, the frequent
striking similarity between the figure of the individual and
that of Israel, as we see it in the community psalms, the

prayer for Zion which suddenly appears in the middle of a psalm for an individual, like Ps. cii (vv. 13–22), the curious vacillation in the text between 'I' and 'we', 'my' and 'our' (cf. Ps. lxxi. 20 [in the *ketib* only—Tr.]; Isa. xxxviii. 20), the transition, often hardly noticeable, from individual to collective prayer (cf. Pss. xii, lxxvii and cxxiii)—all this shows clearly the close relationship to the community even of the individual psalms. The three other characteristics of true prayer only make sense within the framework of the community.

Is *intercession for others* one of these characteristics? Strangely enough, this type of prayer is only found with reference to the king: it is the central theme of the prayer in the royal psalms, Pss. xx and lxxii, and occurs, although it is of secondary importance there, in 1 Sam. ii. 10 and Ps. lxi. 6–7. In the rest of the Old Testament, intercession is basically the task of the prophets (Amos vii. 1–9; Isa. xxxvii. 4; Jer. vii. 16 and elsewhere; cf. also Abraham, Genesis xx. 7; Moses, Num. xxi. 7; Samuel, 1 Sam. vii. 5; and Job xlii. 10). One can only talk of intercession in the psalms, then, in an extremely indirect sense; only through the king, called to be the rightful representative of his people, or by intercession for Israel as a whole, do the psalms contain prayer for others, for one's brothers. Even the prayer against enemies (cf. § 17) is a form of intercession—albeit a strange one to us.

§ 16. Righteous Sinners

We mentioned in the previous section one characteristic of the special style of the psalms, the expression of the lowliness of man in the sight of God. We saw there that this was not simply a matter of a particular attitude, unassuming, and pleasing to God, on the part of man, but rather of something experienced by him, in which the lowliness of his condition plays an essential part.

One particular aspect of this 'lowliness', so characteristic of the psalms, must be described in greater detail. Less frequently than one might expect from the psalms, man's lowliness and humility appears in the form of a confession of his own *sin* and *guilt* or as a petition for *forgiveness*; cf. the seven psalms that in the Middle Ages were actually given the title of 'penitential psalms', namely vi, xxxii, xxxviii, li, cii, cxxx, cxliii and also Pss. xxv. 7; xxxix. 3, 8, 11; xl. 12; xli. 4 and lxix. 5. The point of view from which man is regarded here is clearly 'juristic': when he comes before God he must be 'in the right', that is, he must be 'righteous', if he is lawfully to speak to Him, and thus to be able to pray to Him; and this is why he now confesses that he is *not* a righteous man.

But it would be a mistake to draw the immediate conclusion that according to the psalms the only correct attitude in the sight of God, and therefore the only one pleasing to Him, is that of the penitent confessing his sins. That this is not so is shown by the relative infrequency of such confessions of sin, as well as by the fact that the passages mentioned scarcely go beyond an admission of personal guilt in very general terms (the most precise is Ps. ci. 4–5). We must pay special attention, however, to the confessions of personal *innocence* and *righteousness* which occur in the psalms with striking emphasis and regularity; among the best-known are Pss. xvii. 5, 15; xviii. 20 ff.; xxvi. 1 ff.; xli. 12; lix. 4 f., but they occur in all kinds of different forms—either as an explicit assertion or through the speaker's use of terms such as 'faithful', 'pious', 'honest', 'righteous', or 'servant', '(God's) people', 'his (God's) property'—in virtually every prayer of an individual, of the king and of the community. How can these expressions be reconciled with the admittedly less frequent but no less clearly formulated confessions of personal guilt?

The contradiction that appears to be present here can be explained in different ways. *First*, it is possible that underlying the psalms containing a confession of guilt is a quite different situation from that behind the psalms that speak of the worshipper's innocence; it has been conjectured that in the first case the situation was that of mortal illness, and in the second, of persecution by enemies (e.g., an accusation before a court). Or *secondly*, the two different statements may represent two opposed views of the problem of suffering: on the one hand, a deep consciousness of sin, and on the other a rather naive self-confidence. The *third* possibility is that the contradiction may be explained, and at once reconciled, by the fact that many psalms do confess guilt in the sight of God, but proclaim innocence before men.

None of these attempts at a solution is really satisfactory. The first two cannot explain the fact that apparently contradictory statements frequently occur in one and the same psalm: cf. in Ps. xxxii, v. 5 with vv. 10–11; in Ps. xl, v. 12 with vv. 7–10; in Ps. lxix, v. 4 with v. 11 f.; in Ps. li, vv. 3 ff. with v. 15; in Ps. xli, v. 5 with vv. 7, 9; in Ps. lxxxvi, v. 5 with v. 2; in Ps. cxliii, v. 2 with vv. 8–12, etc. We can at once draw the conclusion that throughout the Psalmists do not see a contradiction, where we suppose that there must be one. There is at least this much truth in the third proposed explanation, that the Psalmists are only concerned with a confession of sin before God (Ps. li. 5); in the face of the 'baseless' persecution of men they know that they are innocent (Ps. vii. 3–5) and righteous before God; or rather one must put it the other way round: because they are first of all righteous in the sight of God, they are therefore also in the right before men. This completely unassailable righteousness in the sight of God, and not their 'good conscience' in the face of every reproach and accusation from men, is the essence of their attitude. Thus the third suggestion also cannot be sustained.

Any credible explanation of this juxtaposition of guilt and innocence must begin with the fact, already noted, that in the mind of the Psalmists the two statements do not contradict but rather complement each other. Because they are righteous before God they confess their guilt to Him, and by means of the confession of the wrong they have done, they become truly righteous. But obviously this righteousness and innocence cannot very well be simply the exact opposite of unrighteousness and guilt; if this were the case, the two statements would immediately exclude each other. It is impossible in the same prayer to express one's guilt and at the same time assert one's innocence!

But according to the psalms, the words 'righteous', 'innocent', 'pious', 'honest', 'faithful', etc., in no way refer to someone who has examined himself and come to the conclusion that they properly describe him. These terms are strictly reserved in the psalms for the 'guests in God's tent' (Ps. xv. 1 ff.; cf. Pss. v and xxiv. 3–6), that is, for all who appear before the face of God and by the imparting of righteousness to them *become* righteous. It is presumed that this imparting of righteousness had its regular place in the worship of Israel—either in the liturgy of the entry into the temple, in the pronouncing of blessing and curse at the conclusion, or elsewhere. The Psalmist can 'rightly' claim this kind of righteousness; he has no need to assert it as though he were one who considered himself righteous. In this context one should no longer speak of *assertions* of innocence, but logically of *confessions* of innocence.

If the righteousness and innocence of the Psalmists is to be explained as resulting from what takes place in worship, this must also be true of their confessions of guilt. For it is the righteous who confess their unrighteousness before God; only the godless man refuses to do this, because he regards himself as righteous. If they are taken in this way, the two statements go together; together they bear witness to the essence of the 'humility', the righteousness of the sinner, which is of value in the sight of God. In the dispute with his friends, so well versed in theology, Job finally makes his point, not because he has successfully asserted his innocence—in so far as he does this, he makes himself unrighteous before God—but because that righteousness is effectively accorded to him.

§ *17. The Wicked Enemies*

One of the best known and at the same time one of the most troublesome features of the Psalter is the extremely prominent part played by godless *enemies*. Who are they? What is their intention? What is the mortal danger with which they threaten the Psalmists? Why are there frequent prayers for their punishment and extermination, but not one for their conversion, or for a reconciliation with them? Is there any place for prayer against enemies even in the Christian community? The Psalter suggests numerous and urgent questions of this nature.

1. Under one or other of the terms that are used for them, these enemies are mentioned in an astonishingly large number of psalms. Lamentation over everything that they attempt to do, prayer against them, thanksgiving that they have been overcome and put to shame, is naturally a regular characteristic of the *royal* psalms. It is also understandable that there are frequent references to enemies in the lamentations and thanksgivings of the *people* or of the *community*. What is quite unexpected is the large part they play in the various categories of *individual* psalms: there are emphatic references to enemies in almost all lamentations, and in many psalms of trust and thanksgiving, and also in the wisdom psalms. In view of the frequency of these references, not to speak of the great prominence that is given to them in particular psalms, it must be admitted that this 'feature' forms part of the essential content of the psalms. It is not possible, then, to handle the problem of these enemies in isolation—far less to commit the impropriety of simply omitting the particularly offensive passages (e.g., Ps. civ. 35 or Ps. cxxxix. 19–22) from Church worship. It is impossible to have the Psalter without its references to godless enemies.

2. From the time of the very earliest interpretations of the psalms—cf. the headings to Pss. xviii, lii, lvi, and lvii—there

have been attempts to ascertain the identity of these enemies, and even, if possible, to learn their names. Since the psalms give a description only in general terms, it is extremely difficult to obtain even a slight degree of certainty. In the royal psalms, of course, one immediately thinks of *foreign* enemies (cf. the heading of Ps. xviii), and even in the lamentations of the people it is not difficult to see in the enemies *foreign oppressors*. But who are the enemies of the *individual*? A number of answers have been given to this question which are worthy of serious consideration. We are told that it must be a question here of enemies '*within*', of 'people of their own nation'. According to this view we should think of personal *adversaries*, *slanderers* and those *envious* of the Psalmist; H. Schmidt thinks of persons who suspect the worshipper of a secret crime on account of his sickness, and are bringing him before a court. S. Mowinckel and others think that the enemies of the individual were originally at least wicked *sorcerers* (in such passages as Pss. vii. 14 ff.; x. 7 ff.). For B. Duhm, who regarded most of the psalms as products of the period of the Maccabees, the enemies were quite simply the *political opponents*, friendly to the Greeks, of the strictly orthodox worshippers. On the basis of the 'poverty' so often lamented by the Psalmists, rich *extortioners*, such as were known at the time of the prophet Amos, have been suggested as a further possibility. In some passages one is even tempted to think of actual *robbers* or of even more dangerous types of criminals.

The choice between these numerous possibilities is made harder by the fact that many details given about these enemies may be intended, wholly or partly, in a *figurative* sense. Usually, therefore, the more modern commentaries hesitate to make an exact identification of the enemies and leave the choice to the reader. It is clear that none of the explanations offered can be true for the whole Psalter.

3. Modern Scandinavian scholars advance the view that the enemies are not human at all, but mythical powers of death. This view expresses the truth, at least, that according

to the psalms there is a material connection between the enemies and death. The charge is made again and again against the enemies that they set traps for the righteous and in fact have sought to bring about their death in every way. The swords, bows and arrows, with which they are armed are in one place called *weapons of death* (Ps. vii. 13), and the images used to describe them (e.g., a ravening and roaring lion, Ps. xxii. 13, etc.) are frequently well-known in the ancient Near East as symbols of death. If God has helped the righteous in time of persecution, his help can easily be described as deliverance 'from death' (cf. Pss. ix. 13; xxx. 1–3; lvi. 13; cxvi. 8 and cxviii. 18).

In spite of all this, however, the enemies are by no means identical with death, nor are they simply the agents and instruments of death. It may well be that—without knowing it—they are carrying on the work of death. But that they are nevertheless to be regarded as ordinary *human beings*, is clear enough from the prayer which asks for their punishment: it desires that they may meet exactly the same fate that they intended 'without a cause' for the righteous (cf. Pss. vii. 12–16; ix. 16; xxxv. 7 f.; cxli. 10, etc.); against demons and mythical powers of death, exorcisms—of the sort that are common in these circumstances in the poetry of Mesopotamia—might be in place, but certainly not a prayer such as this! There is no reason for doubting that these enemies are real human beings.

4. This, however, makes the problem even more acute. The description of the enemies, in the form in which it is often found, particularly in the individual laments, goes in many points beyond the limits of what can be reasonably said of men of flesh and blood even in the exalted language of cultic poetry. For them to be called enemies, adversaries, mockers, liars, hypocrites, robbers, evil-doers, men of blood, blasphemers, godless men, or sinners and be described again and again by epithets such as violent, insolent, evil, false, etc., would still be possible in a description of contemporaries of

the Psalmists. But it becomes difficult to suppose that this is so, when the helpless righteous man is surrounded not by a few enemies, but by an incalculable number at once, and when in one and the same psalm various scarcely reconcilable descriptions and epithets for the enemies are heaped one upon another. Besides this there is the rich variety of images already mentioned, in which the godless are sometimes pictured as an enemy armed with overwhelmingly powerful weapons or as an encircling army, and sometimes as ravenous beasts, as wild oxen, or as a bloodthirsty pack of hounds.

It is obvious that the psalms are describing not a reality that faced righteous men at any particular time, but—apparently—present a picture of the utmost degree of godlessness and violent evil, a picture that already existed for them in the tradition they received. At the same time those who used the psalms in worship had in mind the concrete realities of human life: hypocrites, mockers, slanderers, unbelievers, anti-social landowners, violent abusers of authority, unjust nobles, and presumably evil sorcerers as well; but they followed tradition in portraying them in the exaggerated colours and dimensions of the traditional 'prototype'.

5. What is the source of this conventional and schematic representation of the enemies? It can hardly be that the writers were driven to exaggeration by their passionate feelings, for this is hardly likely in the sacral style of the psalms. If personal experience and feeling had been the decisive factor, the descriptions of the enemies would have contained far more variations, reflecting different reactions to the original provocation. But the descriptions are monotonous, almost schematic; in fact it appears that in the course of time they became more and more monotonous and at the same time more extreme.

In order to explain this remarkable tendency, we can draw attention to a related phenomenon, already discussed in § 16. The figure of the *righteous* is drawn in the psalms in a similar

schematic way, leaving out almost in their entirety any biographical and personal details. The 'extreme' utterances concerning the innocence, poverty, sickness and loneliness of the
righteous constantly go beyond the limits of what is psycho-
logically and biographically possible. It seems right, then, to
understand the figure of the godless *enemy* on the analogy of
the figure of the righteous man, that is, in the light of the
judgement that takes place 'before Yahweh' in the cult. In
this supernatural illumination, only black and white are
visible, the either-or of good and evil: *either* someone is perfect, *or* he is godless—with all that that means. That is
why the Psalmists (e.g., Ps. i) know nothing of those 'intermediate degrees and relative judgements, that are so familiar
to human valuation' (G. von Rad). This is a radical and yet
very merciful view of man, and is the secret of the unshake-
able certainty of the Psalmists!

6. Perhaps this places in a new light the prayers, so offensive to modern feeling, for the *punishment* and *extermination* of
the godless enemies. We must insist that the Psalmists are
concerned with the punishment of real *human beings* and not,
therefore, with a judgement on invisible powers of evil,
represented by a purely poetic device in human and animal
forms. The Psalmists are dealing with men whose total godlessness they have only realised on the basis of the judgement
that has come about in the cult. They are *not* totally godless
for him because of the bitter experience he has of them—
however real this may have been. It is only through the word
pronounced in the cult, proclaiming the will of God as it has
already been revealed in the sacred history of the nation and
bringing it to each individual, that he recognises these enemies as 'absolute' evil-doers hated by God himself, and it is
not till then that he recognises the mortal danger which they
represent for him. It is only this same authoritative word—
and *not*, therefore, his own moral self-valuation—which shows
him that he is a righteous man, in the complete and absolute
sense of which the psalms speak.

The *prayer* of the Psalmist must undoubtedly also be understood against the background of this double legal judgement. If he does not pray on his own account for the reward of his deserving good deeds, how can he pray, in the case of his enemies, for the punishment of any misdeed? The aim of his prayer is the visible *execution* of that judgement: that the *one* will of God should be carried out in its double effect. What the Psalmist prays for is that the judgement of reward and condemnation, already given in the word that has been pronounced, but still only perceptible 'in faith', should *show itself* as a reality. He is concerned with the execution of the righteous will of God, which—according to many statements in the Old Testament—even where it acts as a judgement is wholly and completely His will *to save*, and therefore maintains and renews his *covenant*.

The effect produced on our modern minds by both the form and the content of these prayers is one of strangeness and remoteness. There is no need for this impression to persist, once we have recognised that we are not dealing with outbursts of personal desire for revenge, but with liturgical prayers and formulas, which are directed against the enemies of God in general, and only in a secondary sense against particular adversaries. The influence of the traditional language of the cult—in this case the ancient formulas of cursing, such as were used at the making of the covenant, at the feast of the renewal of the covenant or after the reading of the law— is much wider and more powerful in the psalms than is usually admitted at the present time. If it is the intention of the Christian Church to make a serious use of the psalms in its prayer (cf. § 22), there must now be a new understanding of the strange and remote form they take. But the Church will have to learn above all to utter her prayer for God's will to be done in a new sense, as a prayer for the stern and yet, by the same token, very merciful judgement of God.

§ 18. The Power and the Overthrow of Death

In his famous introduction to the psalms, H. Gunkel says of the individual psalms of lamentation that they are 'the place where the religion of the psalms comes into conflict with death'. In a less well-known comment, O. Noordmans says of this conflict that the psalms are the greatest of all the wonders of the world; for without giving any clear knowledge of the nature of death, 'they have helped one generation after another to pass through death'.

But who is this 'Death', which has already been mentioned in the previous section? Is it to be taken in the psalms as a personal power, or merely as a poetic personification of the common end, ordained by God, of all mortality? As far as the psalms speak of a *conflict* with death, the latter possibility is hardly likely. It is not the necessity of death in itself which is the enemy against whom the Psalmists seek to protect themselves, and against whom they appeal to God for help. For them it is the former 'dynamic' understanding of death which stands in the foreground; 'death' appears to them as a power separate from God, opposed to His rule, and hostile, therefore, in the absolute sense—a power exceeding by far the most terrible human adversaries.

There is no doubt that in this view of death as a personified hostile power we are dealing with one element of a *mythical* view of the world. According to this view the powers and principles which lay down the positive and negative conditions of human life are concentrated in a series of figures who are thought of in supernatural and personal terms, and who, in a decisive drama at the beginning of the world, established all things in the form in which man now experiences them, or is obliged to suffer them. In this view death is also an independent divinity. A Ugaritic myth from the middle of the second millenium B.C., which is characteristic of the spiritual climate of ancient Syria, presents death as the adversary,

victorious at first, but later conquered, of the youthful god
Aleyn Baal. In Canaan proper there also seem to have been
various myths of the victory and the conquest of death; and
there is no need here to comment at any length on the parallels found in Mesopotamia, and above all in Egypt (Osiris
and Seth the god of death). For the nations in the midst of
whom Israel came into being and lived, the whole purpose of
these myths was not merely that of instruction and edifica-
tion: they regarded the events at the beginning of the world,
described in the myths, as being—by virtue of their regular
performance and representation in the cult—a reality that
decided the nature of existence, and guaranteed the existing
order of things.

Israel could not escape the powerful influence of this view
of the world. There are mythical elements in several strata of
the Old Testament; the psalms are no exception to this. One
has only to compare Ps. lxxiv. 13–14;

'Thou didst divide the sea by thy might;
    thou didst break the heads of the dragons on the waters.
Thou didst crush the heads of Leviathan,
    thou didst give him as food for the creatures of the
                                                    wilderness'

and the passage in Isa. li. 9, formally related to it:

'Awake, as in days of old,
    the generations of long ago.
Was it not thou that didst cut Rahab in pieces,
    that didst pierce the dragon?'

This influence is visible not only in individual passages,
but in a tendency that is characteristic of the psalms as a
whole, that is, the rigid 'schematization' of human existence
as a straightforward choice, an 'either-or', between life and
death. When the Psalmists call for the help of God, they are
not seeking the security and enhancement of the life that they
already possess, but the restoration of the life that they have

lost, deliverance *from death* (cf. Pss. xxxiii. 19; lvi. 13; cxvi. 8, etc.). They regard sickness, persecution and other evils of human existence as virtually equivalent to death, as though an 'evil' life simply did not deserve to be called 'life'; and accordingly, to be saved from such an existence signifies for them no less than an escape from death and a return to life. Everything that man enjoys or suffers on earth is judged here by a fixed standard, and recognised either as life or as death. This radical distinction and classification of the phenomena of existence clearly betrays the influence of mythical thinking.

This influence is even more marked in the 'personal' conception of death, which finds expression in certain formulas used in the psalms (especially in the individual psalms of lamentation and thanksgiving). The Psalmists speak of being saved 'from death' or even 'out of the hand', 'out of the power' of death (cf. Pss. xlix. 15; lxxxix. 48). Death is still recognisable here as the *king* of the underworld (Ps. xviii. 5) or as the ravenous *monster* (Isa. v. 14), described in the ancient myths. The same is true of the conception of death as a *kingdom* separated from the rule of God, and hostile to it. Corresponding to the deliverance 'from death' as a personal power, there is the physical delivery 'from the kingdom of death' (Pss. xxx. 3; xlix. 15; lxxxvi. 13; Luther, A.V.: 'from Hell'). He who is accursed or exiled, sick or in prison, wandering in the desert and in peril at sea (Ps. cvii)—all these are already 'in the kingdom of death', and are comparable to those who have long been in the grave (Pss. lxxxviii. 5-7; xxii. 15; Lam. iii. 53-55; cf. Pss. xxx. 3; ciii. 4; Jonah ii. 7). All life is threatened by death—as by a kingdom hungry for land—and placed under its curse. Mythical thinking is visible here in the fact that the phenomena which bear the stamp of evil are classified and localised in space and time; this conception was expressed and reinforced in the cultic representation of the periodic dying and restoration to life of nature.

Further evidence is provided by the way in which the redeeming *act of God* is often described. The worshipper is not

delivered from death simply by an authoritative pronounce-
ment; it often seems as if Yahweh has first to awake, arrive,
march out or come down and—a decisive point—fight and
conquer in a battle, before the deliverance is brought about,
cf. Pss. xvii. 13 f.; xxxv. 1 ff.; lv. 23; lxviii. 1 ff. and the
powerful descriptions in Pss. xviii and cxliv. Are these simply
'military images', examples of the imitation of the style of
the royal psalms? Probably they are distant echoes of the
story of a struggle between life and death at the beginning
of the world, which, to judge by Ps. lxxiv. 13 f.; Job. xxvi.
12; Isa. li. 9 f., was still clearly recollected in Israel even at a
later period.

Finally the fact ought to be mentioned that, according to
the psalms, it is not a matter of indifference which men have
to undertake the conflict with death: it is always those who
are in the fullest sense alive, God's chosen, the *righteous*—
and often even his special representatives, the *kings*—who
have to tread the way, at once terrible and glorious, through
suffering and death to new life. The deliverance of the individual from the power of death is important as an example for
the community as a whole (Ps. xxx. 4 f.), and indeed for 'all
the ends of the earth' (xxii. 27); that the hearts of those who
are oppressed should 'revive', when they hear of this deliverance (xxii. 26; lxix. 32), appears to presuppose a real
participation by the many in the experience of the one individual. This rather seems to point to a comparison with what
takes place in the cultic dramas of the vegetation rites (Osiris,
Adonis, Tammuz, etc.).

But in establishing that there are powerful reminiscences
of the ancient myths still present in the psalms, we have not
yet come to the main point. The Israelites took over a great
deal from their environment, but were never completely
conformed to it. In the psalms, no single myth of the conquest
of death is preserved 'intact'; what we have referred to above
have been fragments and echoes, purely formal similarities.

At the most important points these myths were robbed of their real content, and what was left was used to bear witness to a 'conquest of death' of a different nature (cf. B. S. Childs, *Myth and Reality in the Old Testament,* 1960).

This is first of all visible in the fact that the psalms do not accord to death the *divine* honour and status which it undoubtedly possessed in the older view. Although the language of the psalms, tied as it is to tradition, still presents death as a personal power existing in space and time, yet it is clearly no longer allowed to play the part of an equal to God. The faith of Israel provides no legitimate place for such a being, and conceives of death as a reality powerful enough in its manifestation, but relegated even more powerfully by the act of God into the realm of past realities. Thus Israel recognises the threat presented by death to the unique sovereignty of God, while still refusing to accord this threat any respect as a legitimate element of the present world order. This gives no 'clear knowledge of the nature of death'—cf. the comment of O. Noordmans mentioned at the beginning of this section; but the psalms are clear to this extent, that they consciously reject any consistent mythical picture of death.

Secondly, the psalms show their independence by the sober *historical* sense in which they conceive of the event of deliverance from death. There are passages in the psalms where the conquest of death is presented as an event which has taken place more than once in the past (Pss. xxxiii. 18 f.; lxviii. 21). But they are astonishingly consistent in not basing this victory of life, as the myths would, on an event that happened at the beginning of time, that is *before and outside* history; they avoid analogies to the natural cycle of life and death, and never make allusion to the cultic repetition and appropriation to the present of that timeless event. Even where Yahweh is described in archaic language as a warrior and heroic victor, there is a tendency to 'historicize' by the substitution of a tangible human and historical enemy in place of the power of death that was his original opponent, cf. Pss. xvii, xxxv, and cxliv. A characteristic example of this is the gradual transformation of the sea dragon Rahab (Ps. lxxxix. 10; Job ix. 13; xxvi. 12; Isa. li. 9 f.) into a poetic name for Egypt (Ps. lxxxvii. 4; Isa. xxx. 7). This tendency to historicization is also recognizable by the fact that Yahweh—unlike the dying god Baal—is never presented as the personal subject of suffering in the struggle with death, but only in an indirect and mediated way. He only appears as such, in fact, in so far as he 'adopts' the historical Israelite nation (Exod. iv. 22; Hosea xi. 1), the kings, (2 Sam. vii. 14; Pss. ii. 7; lxxxix. 26 f.) and with them the individual members of the nation, thus making their distress his own. In this way the conquest of death becomes no longer an element of the existing world order, laid down from the beginning of time, but is more and more clearly seen as an historical act of God breaking into this order.

Finally, the psalms show their independence by their endeavour to understand the conquest of death in relationship to the *faith of Israel*. When they talk of the restoration of life, they admittedly include the prosperity and survival of the created world, which was the purpose of the myth, but this is far from being all that they are thinking of. In the psalms 'life' means a share in the land and the promises of Israel (Ps. xvi), membership of the chosen people in the 'land of the living' apportioned to them (Ps. xxvii. 13), and the right to live and die in righteousness, as defined by the covenant founded and ratified by Yahweh (Num. xxiii. 10). In this context 'death' means the opposite, an allotted place far away from God (Ps. lxxiii. 23–28), exclusion from taking part in his praise (Pss. vi. 5; xxx. 9; lxxxviii. 11 f.; cxv. 17; Isa. xxxviii. 18). 'Life' for the psalms means the historical formation and appearance of the people of God, while 'death' means their sinking back into the natural existence of the heathen, fundamentally without history. It is true that the Psalmists hope for an 'eternal' life 'in the land of the living'; but it should be observed that by this they mean *not a continuation* of temporal existence on earth, but its radical *re-*

newal through true life, the life repeatedly described in Ps. lxxiii (vv. 23, 25, 28) as 'being near to God'.

Thus the *conquest of death* to which the psalms bear witness is in fact of an 'other-worldly' nature. It is not based on the nature and potentialities of the world, and, within the world, of man, as laid down from all eternity, nor does it consist in bringing these to perfection. It is brought about by the free acts of God in His Faithfulness, whereby He calls, establishes and maintains individual men—despite their own powerlessness—as members of His people.

§ 19. The Fundamentals of Faith

In the last few sections we have sought to comprehend the characteristic nature of the psalms from different points of view; we inquired in turn into the question of true prayer, of the innocence of the Psalmist, of the identity of the enemies, and of the conquest of death. Each time we saw that these questions—chosen to provide a few typical examples— were answered in the psalms on the basis of a definite *faith*.

Of course in a collection of prayers, songs and poems from at least six centuries, such as we find in the Psalter, we cannot expect a unified system of doctrine or confession of faith: the liturgies of the sacred federation of the tribes (Pss. l and lxxxi) do not seem to have much in common with the court poetry of Zion (Pss. ii, cx, lxxxix, and cxxxii), while the festal hymn, Ps. xxix, with its many Canaanite features, is poles apart from the grim lyric in Ps. cxxxvii. But in spite of many differences of a 'dogmatic' kind there is no doubt that the psalms have a common basis. We shall try to describe it at least in outline.

We must first make a comment on the meaning of the word *faith*. In modern usage it oftens means no more than 'belief', the reasonable acceptance of a fact; we believe that an account or proposition is true or at least probable. The biblical usage is quite different. The meaning of the expressions used for 'faith' is in the first place the *trust* accorded to a *person;* only in consequence of this do they refer to the belief placed in that person's words and other ideas expressed by his action; the language of the Bible lacks any expression for the acceptance of impersonal truths and possibilities—just as though there were no such thing!

In this sense the faith to which the psalms bear witness is also entirely 'personal'; the common basis of all the psalms is a constant, total and exclusive trust in the God of Israel. The speech and song, rejoicing and lamentation, prayer and thanksgiving of the psalms flows from this trust, and seeks to find it again. But where does this trust come from? It certainly does not spring up by accident.

1. According to the psalms, the origin of this trust in the God of Israel lies in certain historical acts of God. When we talk of *historical* acts, we mean that they were events which once *happened* in the history of particular men and nations, and in consequence were *seen, understood* and *handed down* to posterity. Through accounts of such acts the faith of Israel came into being and grew; the same accounts nourished and renewed it as time went on (cf. Ps. lxxviii. 2–7). The faith of Israel is firmly based on the fact that these acts of God took place, that everybody can learn about them, and that they can be constantly re-told. Without the 'great' and 'wonderful works' of God (Pss. lxxi. 19; lxvi. 3; cvi. 22, etc.) there would be no trust in God in the psalms. God is a 'rock', 'fortress' and 'refuge' (Pss. xviii. 3; xlvi. 2, etc.) for Israel, not because of the timeless and enduring perfection of His being, but in the first and principal instance, in and through His acts: it is through them that He reveals Himself as a rock, a fortress and a refuge.

So these acts are not simply evidence to strengthen the faith of Israel, and signs of the perfection of God; they are at the same time, and to a much more significant extent, facts that *arouse* trust and provide the objective *basis* of faith, self-evident facts which admit of no doubt.

The trust in God that is also expressed in the parallel literature to the psalms outside the Bible (§ 13) has no such roots in history. Instead, it is based on the action of the myth, the whole point of which is that it did not take place once for all, and which guaranteed the maintenance for ever of the natural order of the world, as well as its continued renewal and renovation. According to A. Weiser the faith of the Old Testament is 'only clearly understood when the influence that history has had on the development of this faith is recognised'. But it is not history or particular historical events in themselves which gave rise to the faith of Israel and formed it, but the acts of God *within* history. Israel sees the hand of God at work precisely where the course of history has been miraculously interrupted, altered and diverted, and where the powers and laws that govern history have to yield to a new reality created by God. As the irruption of this new reality, totally without parallel (Pss. xl. 6; lxxi. 19; lxxxvi. 8), these acts of God are able to provide the substance and the assurance of the faith of Israel.

2. The acts of God in history which provide the foundation of Israel's faith are unique, according to the psalms, because they are essentially works of *salvation*. They are called 'great' 'marvellous', 'glorious', 'mighty' and 'terrible' partly in contrast with what history has previously known (Exod. xv. 11), but even more on account of their own nature. We term them 'works of salvation', although there is no exactly equivalent Hebrew word—the corresponding Biblical expressions speak of acts of 'righteousness' and 'deliverance', of 'faithfulness' and 'steadfastness'—and although the word 'salvation' can lead to numerous misunderstandings. By his acts God works salvation, in the sense that He lets justice and redemption come to men—not for any claim that man can make, but from an obligation to man which He takes on of His own free will, and from faithfulness to Himself. However, that in *all*

His acts—that is, not only where He is clearly bringing blessing, assistance, protection, deliverance, freedom, redemption
and forgiveness, but equally in His avenging anger—God is
bringing salvation, and nothing else, was a truth the Psalmists
could never assume as a truism. Psalms such as lxxxix, lxxvii,
xliv and lxxxv have to wrestle with the question of whether
God's avenging righteousness can be reconciled with the
mercy He has always shown Israel in the past (cf. Pss. lxxxix.
49; lxxvii. 6–13; lxxxv. 4–7; cxliii. 5); is God not actually
doing *evil* here, and does this not mean that He is contradic-
ting His own words and name? The appeal to the faithfulness
of God, which forms the climax to many of these psalms, especially the psalms of lamentation, shows clearly where they
look for the answer: in His loving kindness, which endures for
ever, and also in His anger, which only lasts for a moment
(Pss. xxx. 5, cf. Exod. xx. 5–6; Isa. liv. 7–8), He is 'the God of
our salvation' (Ps. lxxxv. 4). But a human understanding,
surveying the work of God as a unity, and seeing His
anger and His loving kindness as complementary, cannot give
an authoritative answer to this question; God Himself gives
it in constant new assurances of His faithfulness (cf. 2 Sam. vii.
23 ff., 1 Chron. xvii. 21 ff.). For the acts of God in the past
are recognised and become effective as acts of *salvation*, able
to inspire and maintain faith in the midst of the temptations
of the present time, only when a further act of God proves
them to be so (Ps. lxxxix. 49). The faith of Israel lives in the
expectation of such an 'assurance' of what has happened in
the past.

3. But which are the acts and deeds of God on which the
faith of Israel is based? The Psalter provides fuller information on this matter than any book in the Bible. This faith is
not based on everything that God has done in his providence,
but only on a *selection* of His acts; a selection that at first sight
is confusing in its complexity, but on closer examination soon
appears meaningful and consistent. It only includes such acts
of God which in a more or less direct sense led to the coming

into being and continued existence of the historical reality known as 'Israel'. That is why it is principally the very earliest period or—to use an expression typical of the prophets (but cf. also Ps. cxxix. 1–2)—the 'youth' of Israel, which is considered in this context: the oppression and the Exodus from Egypt, the miracle at the Red Sea and the forty years in the wilderness, the revelation at Sinai and finally the entry into the promised land. These themes are treated in great detail in the so-called 'history of salvation' psalms (Exod. xv; Deut. xxxii; Pss. lxxviii, cv, cvi, cxi, cxiv, cxxxv, cxxxvi), and even where the acts of God are recalled more incidentally, they are clearly the most prominent (Pss. xliv, l, lxvi, lxviii, lxxiv, lxxvii, lxxx, lxxxi, lxxxiii, xcv, xcix and ciii).

It is surprising that the stories of the *patriarchs*, which one might suppose from the book of Genesis would be regarded as an important act in the drama of the making of Israel, are only celebrated in one psalm, Ps. cv. The place given in the psalms to the proclamation of the law at *Sinai* is strikingly modest by comparison with God's other acts of salvation (Pss. xcix, ciii, cvi, but *not* in Pss. lxxviii, cv, cxxxv, cxxxvi). As for the acts of God after the entry in Canaan, the psalms seem in practice to regard only the choice and institution of *David* as king to be of fundamental importance (Pss. lxxxix, cxxxii, lxxviii. 65–72), although this same covenant with David is often presented as the ultimate development of the old covenant 'from Egypt' (cf. Pss. lxxviii. 67 ff.; xviii. 16 and the linking together of the traditions of David and of Sinai in Pss. xviii. 20–24; lxxii. 1–7; ci and cxxxii); thus the history of David is treated as part of the 'youth' of Israel, not in a chronological sense, but as regards its essential significance.

An apparent exception from this rule is the praise of God as *creator*, so characteristic of the psalms, cf. the well-known 'nature psalms', viii, xix and civ, with which festival hymns such as Pss. xxix, xxxiii, xciii, xcv, cxxxvi and cxlviii, as well as a series of scattered references in psalms of different categories (Ps. xxiv. 1 f.; lxxiv. 12–17; lxxxix. 5–12; xc. 2; xcvi.

5; cxv. 15; cxix. 90; cxxiv. 8; cxxxiv. 3; cxlvi. 6) must also be taken into account. It appears that we have here an independent article of faith, separate from the 'birth' and 'youth' of Israel. But appearances are deceptive. Even in His work of creation God is at work to bring into being the reality that is called 'Israel'. This explains what is for us a most remarkable combination, a hymn ('the heavens are telling the glory of the Lord') occuring together with the prayer of an individual worshipper ('the law of the Lord is perfect') in Ps. xix. Several of the psalms—especially Pss. lxxxix. 5–12; lxxiv. 12–17; cxxxvi. 5–9; cxlviii. 1–13—agree with Deutero-Isaiah (Isa. xl. 21 ff.; xliv. 24 ff.; xlv. 11 ff.; li. 9 ff.; liv. 5), and with the two accounts of the creation in Genesis i–ii, in regarding the creation of the *world* as being one stage in the creation of *Israel*. 'Creation' does not merely mean here 'bringing into existence'; it also means the limiting of the powers of chaos and evil that threaten all creation (cf. Gen. i), and therefore implies the deliverance, preservation, and, as a direct consequence, the ruling and governing of the creation. It is clear that what God has done in the *world*, is, according to the psalms, most closely related to what He has done with regard to *Israel*, in which in fact the creation of the world first receives its true meaning. The meaning of the history of the *world* is found in the history of *salvation*, while the history of salvation in turn can only be properly understood as a revelation and unveiling of the meaning of the history of the world.

Thus the one act of God on which the faith of Israel is based is the creation of that very reality which is called Israel. This does not in any sense mean that Israel believed 'in itself' as a human community created once for all by God, and from then on preserved by Him. The foundation and object of Israelite faith, of course, is the 'real' Israel. (cf. G. von Rad, *Old Testament Theology*, (E.T.), vol. I (1962) p. 118). But of what does the reality of the people of God consist?

Neither the empirical Israel that has existed throughout the centuries down to the present day, nor an ideal of the true Israel to be looked for beyond this empirical phenomenon, can be equated with the reality of Israel in the sense of the psalms. We cannot speak of this reality, the 'real' Israel, except in relation to God Who brought Israel into being, and Whose work is still in progress. He is part of the reality which is the object of Israel's faith. That this is so, is shown by the pregnant confessional formula of Ps. c. 3: 'Know that the Lord is God! It is he that made us, and we are his; we are his people and the sheep of his pasture'. As an entity 'brought about' by God—when He created, chose, called, gathered together, set free and showed mercy on the nation—Israel came into being, and received a share in God's own reality; and only in this way can Israel carry out the work intended for the nation by God, of acknowledging Him and confessing Him in faith. Faith in the real Israel is only one aspect of faith in the God of Israel, and in His work in history. The real Israel only exists in faith in *this* God and in *this* work; but to believe in Him and His work thus means, in fact, believing in the true Israel as well. Looking away from itself towards its Creator—constantly hoping, expecting, and trusting—Israel shows again and again that it is the people of God, which before all other nations is called to honour Him. The psalms are an example of this that is valid for all time.

§ 20. David, the Royal Psalmist

When words from the Psalter are quoted in the New Testament, it is frequently taken for granted that they are none other than the words of David, the servant of God and the king of Israel (e.g., Matt. xxii. 43; Luke xx. 42; Acts. i. 16; iv. 25; Romans iv. 6; Heb. iv. 7). David is regarded as *the* Psalmist, just as Moses is regarded as *the* law-giver and Solomon *the* man of wisdom, cf. § 5. We are used to seeing the

results of this conception in pictures of Moses with the rays
about his face and the tablets of the law in his hand, and of
David as a crowned king with his harp. This traditional picture of David is the final stage in a development which took
a thousand years. In its early stages David's intimate connection with the psalms was by no means so prominent.

1. In the long collection of stories of David's rise from a
simple shepherd boy to be king over all Israel (1 Sam. xv.
14–2 Sam. v. 25) there are two apparently independent traditions of the events which led to the discovery and advance-
ment of David. According to the first story (1 Sam. xvii. 1–
58; xviii. 2) David, until that time unknown to the king
(xvii. 58), came to court as the conqueror of Goliath, and was
very soon made commander of the army (xviii. 5). According
to the other account, which is the important one for us (xvi.
14–23) Saul was looking for a man 'who was skilful in *playing
the lyre*', and (on the recommendation of a courtier) found
such a person in David. Although neither singing nor com-
posing poetry is mentioned here, this account seems to provide the origin of the later tradition of David, the royal
Psalmist. As early as the eighth century, Amos, a prophet
from Judah, mentions this tradition, and in fact takes for
granted that everyone (even in the northern kingdom) is
acquainted with it. Amos is prophesying against the nobles
of Zion and Samaria, 'who sing idle songs to the sound of the
harp, and like David invent for themselves instruments of
music' (Amos vi. 5; some translations have 'compose songs').
A further stage in the development of the tradition can be
seen in the books of Chronicles, where the climax of an ex-
tended description of David's reign (1 Chron. xi–xxix) is an
account of the organisation of worship in the temple (Ch.
xiii; xv–xvi; xxi–xxix) and the climax of this in its turn is the
ordering of the praise of God (Ch. xv, xvi, xxv, xxix). David
clearly appears (cf. e.g., xvi. 7) as the initiator and organiser
of the singing of psalms. According to 1 Chron. xxiii. 4, and
2 Chron. xxix. 26 f. he made himself personally responsible

for the provision of the necessary instruments, and in fact even gave instructions for their use (1 Chron. xxv. 2, 6), which remained in force even after his death (2 Chron. xxiii. 6; Ezra iii. 10). The account in 2 Chron. xxix. 30, where Hezekiah commands the praise of God to be sung 'with the words of David' could be regarded as the first reference to David as the author of psalms, but on the analogy of 2 Chron. xxix. 15, and in accordance with Hebrew usage, (cf. 2 Chron. xxi. 19; Esth. i. 12), this phrase should in fact be translated here 'according to David's words'—that is, 'regulations'. It is in the Greek translation of 2 Chron. xxiii. 18; xxix. 30; Ezra iii. 10, which was followed by Luther and many more recent translations, that the idea is first clearly expressed that David *composed* and *wrote* psalms. The headings to the psalms, then, which present David as the author—with exact biographical details!—cannot have been written before the third century B.C., cf. § 4 above, and 2 Sam. xxii. 1; the note 'a psalm of David', which occurs at the head of seventy-three of the psalms, was presumably not taken to mean that he was their author until this period. The view held in the Church from the beginning, right up to the nineteenth century, that David composed *all* the psalms, seems to occur first in the Talmud (R. Meir, Pesachim 117a, as quoted by Fr. Delitzsch).

2. The very close connection of David with the psalms, however, is not based simply on the older and more recent traditions concerning his musical and liturgical gifts and activities. It was not simply as 'God's minstrel' that he became the royal Psalmist! Just as important, and perhaps even more important in this respect, is David's exalted status as the *servant of God* and *king of Israel*. Even when he was alive he seems to have attained a unique importance for the faith of Israel. When we consider what has been learned in the last few decades about the 'sacral kingship' of the ancient Near East, it is not surprising that his reign was seen as surrounded by the light of a special, divine consecration and distinction, cf. § 11 above. But it is still astonishing that a king should

come to have a fixed place in the faith of Israel—where a human kingdom was originally unknown—and that this king should be called by no other name but David, although there were others of some importance who filled his office. His unusual wisdom as a statesman, his outstanding military ability, and the splendour and vast extent of his kingdom may have contributed towards the special position which he was accorded; but all this is insufficient to explain how his kingdom came to be included among the essential elements of the faith of Israel (cf. § 19, 3).

The reason for this is probably to be sought in the traditions concerning David's life. In everything that he did and suffered as a shepherd boy, armour bearer, leader of mercenaries and king, and by the kind of man he showed himself to be in all these roles, he is regarded by these traditions as typical of Israel as a whole. His own life was unique, but it reflected something of the unworthiness and the choosing, the suffering and triumph, and poverty and greatness of *Israel*. It is not without reason that David is regularly described as the man who brought the Ark of the Covenant to Jerusalem, thus basing the kingdom on the choosing of Israel from the period of Egypt and Sinai onwards (2 Sam. vi; 1 Chron. xiii, xv, xvi; Ps. cxxxii), and there is good reason too why his name should be connected in the earlier period and later with titles which—conferred in such concentration only on him—describe him as an archetype for all Israel: as God's *chosen* (2 Sam. vi. 21; 1 Kings viii. 16; xi. 34; Ps. lxxxix. 3), as the *anointed* of the God of Jacob (2 Sam. xxiii. 1; Ps. cxxxii. 10, 17) and as the *servant of Yahweh* (2 Sam. viii, *passim*; Pss. lxxxix. 3, 20; cxxxii. 10; lxxviii. 70; xviii. 1; xxxvi. 1; Ezek. xxxiv. 23; xxxvii. 25). In this representative character he came to be of importance for the worshipping life of Israel: not only for the ritual of the court (Pss. xviii, lxxxix, cxxxii), but also— as can be easily seen from Pss. lxxviii. 69; cxxii. 5; Isa. xxxvii. 35; 2 Kings viii. 19; xix. 34; xx. 6—for the worship of the Jewish community. And it was a natural result that (according to Isa. lv. 3–5) the 'new' covenant of God with the remnant of Israel should be based on God's faithfulness to David.

Perhaps the somewhat obscure title given to David at the end of 2 Sam. xxiii. 1 ('the sweet psalmist of Israel', R.S.V.; 'the favourite of the songs of Israel', R.S.V. margin) should be taken to mean that as a leading and archetypal figure in Israel David had become the favourite *subject* of the songs of Israel. As the Jewish community prayed and recited the psalms, they may have recalled the talented minstrel of God; but their memory dwelt no less on the king, pursued and abandoned in innocence and guilt, but always delivered and restored to power by the faithfulness of God, in whom their own existence as the people of God had found an expression that was valid for all time. Considering that no later than the period immediately after the fall of Jerusalem (cf. Hosea iii. 5; Amos ix. 11; Jer. xxiii. 5; xxx. 9; xxxiii. 15, 17, 21; Ezek. xxxiv. 23 f.; xxxvii. 24 f.) the remnant of Israel hoped for David's *return*, there is every reason to suppose that as the Jewish community prayed the psalms they thought of David with at least an equally firm *hope* and *expectation*.

Thus David became 'the royal psalmist' in two different ways—as the minstrel and as the servant of God. It would be a worthwhile task to enquire whether and to what degree these two strands of the tradition influenced and strengthened each other. This inquiry would also need to go into the question whether and to what extent the central and northern tribes, as well as the later Samaritan community, which as is well-known had 'no part in David' (2 Sam. xii. 16; 1 Kings xi. 16) were nevertheless able—especially in their worship—to be and to remain the chosen people of Yahweh.

§ 21. Jesus Christ in the Psalter

It is a well-known fact that neither the name *Jesus* nor His title *Christ* occur in the psalms. However late the date of completion of the Psalter is set, it is bound to have taken place in pre-Christian times, when no one could know anything of Jesus of Nazareth. The title Christ (and the corresponding Hebrew term *mashiach*, transcribed in Greek as *Messias*) was in fact used in the Psalter for the 'anointed' kings of Israel and Judah, but it does not occur on a single occasion with the full significance which it came to carry in late Jewish writings and in the New Testament. Thus Jesus Christ is apparently unknown in the Book of Psalms.

But this bare fact is not the final word. According to what is said in the New Testament, that is, by the Apostles and by the early Christian Church, there is a profound relationship between Jesus Christ and the psalms, both as regards his person and the events of his earthly life. According to their interpretation and witness, the Psalter frequently speaks about Jesus Christ—about his humiliation and exaltation, his suffering and endurance, his death and resurrection; they frequently find in the Psalter the very words of Jesus Christ (cf. the story of the Passion; Matt. vii. 23; Romans xv. 3, etc.). For them, the essential message of the Psalter—as of the rest of the Old Testament—is a witness to Jesus Christ. What is the explanation of this astonishing fact, and how is it related to what was said at the beginning of the section?

Some difficulty is presented by the seemingly arbitrary way in which the New Testament writers read and expounded the Psalter. Their quotations from this book (cf. C. H. Dodd, *According to the Scriptures*, 1952) usually follow one of the old Greek translations and sometimes they may be made from memory, so that they often show not inconsiderable departures from the wording and sense of the Hebrew original (e.g., Ps. xvi. 10, in Acts ii. 27 and xiii. 33).

Further, it becomes obvious that whenever it is a question of a decisive witness to the words and the work of Jesus Christ, the New Testament draws on a relatively small *selection* of psalms; the coronation liturgies Pss. ii and cx, the individual lamentations Pss. xxii and lxix, the hymn Ps. viii, the prayer of trust Ps. xvi, and the festal liturgy of thanksgiving Ps. cxviii are quoted again and again, or alluded to more or less clearly.

It has also been noticed that in the choice of the passages in the psalms which they relate to Jesus, the Messiah, the New Testament authors are often strongly influenced by the occurrence of certain *key words*, known to them from the oldest, perhaps still unwritten tradition concerning Jesus. The mention of the words 'anointed' and 'son' in Ps. ii. 2, 7, or of the 'son of man' (taken to mean the exalted 'Son of Man' of apocalyptic) in Pss. viii. 4, 6, and lxxx. 17, as well as of the *Kyrios* ('Lord') in Ps. xxxiv. 9, seems to have been the primary occasion for the use of these passages as a witness to Jesus, the Son of God and Son of Man, the Christ and Lord (cf. Acts iv. 25 f.; xiii. 33; Heb. i. 5; v. 5; 2 Peter i. 17; Matt. xxi. 16; Heb. ii. 6–9; 1 Cor. xv. 27; 1 Peter ii. 3; cf. also Heb. i. 6 with Ps. xcvii. 7).

Finally, it is astonishing to see how such key words, and also often whole verses and longer passages, are lifted from their own context and have a 'messianic' interpretation imposed upon them; historical kings of Judah (Pss. ii, cx), unknown individuals (Pss. xxii and lxix), man as such, in the way Israel regarded him (Ps. viii), or Yahweh, the God of Israel, Himself (Pss. xxxiv. 8; xcvii. 7) were originally referred to in passages where the New Testament sees a testimony to Jesus the Messiah!

This way of handling the psalms can not in fact be reconciled with the principles of scientific Biblical exegesis. But to apply such a modern standard to the work of the apostolic and the post-apostolic generation is itself a mistake. At that time it was not easy to have access to the text of holy scripture, and in addition, only a few could understand it in its Hebrew form; there was still no 'authorised' version, and innumerable variations in the reading and interpretation of the text were unavoidable.

The best explanation for the relatively small number of
psalms that are used for this purpose is probably that the
application of the psalms to Jesus the Messiah, like every
other new departure in exegesis, would be based at the beginning on certain particularly appropriate texts; the Church
then went on to apply the same principle in other texts, as
can be seen in the post-apostolic generation (the Epistle to
the Hebrews), and even more so at a later period (although
with varying success).

With regard to the use of key words by the New Testament
in the choice of passages referring to Jesus Christ (Luke xxiv.
44–47), a note of special caution must be sounded; as a rule,
it was not the Christians of the early Church who sought and
discovered their own ideas and conceptions of Jesus in the
scriptures, but rather the scriptures which supplied the early
Church with the conceptual equipment with which to
achieve an adequate understanding of the history of Jesus
and to reproduce it in story and sermon. Far from serving
merely as 'proof texts', these scriptures—pre-eminent among
them the psalms and the Book of Isaiah—gave a definitive
form to our whole picture of Jesus, 'the Son of God' and
'Son of Man', the 'Lord' and 'king', the 'Servant of God' and
'Priest', the 'man on the right hand of God', etc. In this sense
the application of appropriate quotations is anything but a
play upon words.

Finally, the criticism that the application of certain passages to Christ ignores the context and therefore the original
meaning of the text used, cannot be entirely repudiated;
there are in fact passages in which either the text of the Old
Testament on which the interpretation was based (e.g., Pss.
cx. 1; and xvi. 10) or quite simply the state at that time of
exegetical and historical knowledge (e.g., Ps. viii. 4–6) pre-
vented a correct understanding of the original sense. But as
C. H. Dodd, op. cit., p. 67 ff. has shown, there can be no
question of the conscious uprooting of single words or verses
from their context, far less of the wilful alteration of the

meaning of a text of scripture from the sense in which it was accepted. It is noteworthy how Peter in Acts ii. 25 ff., and Paul in xiii. 35 ff. understand and appreciate the 'historical' sense of Ps. xvi. 8–10 in the context of that psalm, although the psalm is taken as a prophecy of Christ! The Apostles are convinced that not merely a few isolated words, but the whole context which they represent, taken in what to the best of their knowledge was its proper meaning, speaks of Jesus, the Messiah.

But how did they come to find in the psalms the very words of Jesus, and clear references to Him? At that time, as today, it was possible to read the psalms without taking their words in this sense. As we have already noticed, it was a case of a 'new departure' in exegesis, but nothing suggests that this was due to a new method of exegesis, such as the allegorical or spiritual interpretations which came into use later, which were based on the doctrine of the multiple sense of scripture. According to Luke xxiv. 25–27 and 44–48, Jesus, risen from the dead, opened the minds of His disciples 'to understand the scriptures' (cf. John xx. 9). This was the way, and this was the first moment, that the discovery of what the psalms said 'concerning him', was introduced. Not until the resurrection of Jesus, that is, until the conclusion of his historical work, was it possible to hear and understand the message of the psalms concerning Jesus. Here the understanding of the scriptures is not an aim in itself, but an indispensable means towards the understanding of the life and historical acts of Jesus, which otherwise would be altogether incomprehensible: only through the witness of the scriptures (John v. 39) is Jesus recognised as the person He is in reality.

But of what, then, does this indispensable and authoritative revelation of the scriptures—in our case, of the psalms— concerning the meaning of the life and work of Jesus, in fact consist? It is certainly not sufficient to answer that the psalms *predicted* or *foretold* His life—in broad outline or even in specific detail. Actually, they speak of the history and reality of

Israel (cf. § 19, 3). After the conclusion of Jesus' earthly life
and work, however, it was suddenly recognised that they
had something else to say. Along with their witness to the
history and reality of Israel, they bore, and still bear, witness
to the life and work of *Jesus*. The Psalms now reveal the
meaning of this life and work. They show that Jesus and
Israel belong together, and that their respective histories cannot be understood apart from each other. This they do by
making evident the close and essential similarity between the
history of Israel and the life of Jesus, showing that they are in
fact one and the same: it is the story of God's dwelling with
His people, or to put it the other way round, the dwelling of
this people with their God. This story, and this story alone, is
brought to its conclusion, 'to its fulfilment', with the life and
work of Jesus.

For this is the subject of the psalms: God, who in love or
anger, forgiveness or punishment, seeks to be God only as the
God of Israel, and Israel, which can only exist as the people
of this God. God and man are involved with each other in
this history in the most marvellous way, without God's ceas-
ing to be God, and without man becoming more then he—a
mere creature, Ps. viii—is in fact capable of being. How
God comes to man, to walk beside him, and how man is
exalted 'to the right hand of God' is described and explained
in the psalms before it is brought to fulfilment and consum-
mation in the life and work of Jesus. By their own admission,
the Apostles would not have been able to speak so clearly and
with such authority about Jesus, even as a result of the most
complete revelation.

In the psalms the voice of Israel is heard, and through it
the voice of God. These voices must be distinguished and each
received for what it is; but it is wrong to separate them, and
to try to hear one without the other. For by the very fact
that they are both heard together, they bear witness to the
presence of God amongst men, and of man with God. Thus

the psalms 'mediate' to us the voice of Jesus, for through them we learn to understand that He is God, unapproachable in His holiness and yet full of condescension, and that at the same time He is man, forlorn and abandoned, and yet exalted beyond all understanding.

It is true that the Apostles perceived the voice of Jesus—or a testimony to Him—only in particular psalms. We look in vain in the New Testament for a systematic method which would simply *equate* the voice of Yahweh on the one hand, and on the other hand the voice of Israel, of Israel's kings and of unknown worshippers, with the voice of Jesus, so that His voice would be perceived in practically every psalm. The Apostles preferred to make use of the psalms in which the close relationship between God and man was so clearly visible that it was impossible that the *Kyrios* (e.g., Ps. xxxiv. 9) could simply mean 'God in Himself', or that the 'son of man' (e.g., Ps. viii) could simply refer to man in himself. On the other hand this limited use does not imply that on principle the Apostles might not have looked in every psalm for the same testimony to Jesus, the Messiah. The New Testament provides only a few examples of the service which the psalms were able to render to the Church. It is certain that with the present state of our knowledge about their historical meaning, they have much more to offer both to the Church, and also to Israel itself, the Synagogue.

§ 22. The Psalms in the Worship of the Church

Like the whole Old Testament, the Psalter has also a definite and vital function to fulfil in the Church. Without the Old Testament and without the Psalter the Church would not be the people of God, called from afar off (Acts ii. 39; Rom. ii. 26; Eph. ii. 13), and now included in the old Israel. But what is the particular function of the Psalter?

As far as one can see, Christianity very soon made its own

use of the Psalter, as the 'hymn book and prayer book of the Old Testament Church'. Whether this was true as early as the apostolic period is not quite so certain as is usually assumed; for St. Paul's injunction: 'address one another in psalms and hymns and spiritual songs, singing and making melody to the Lord with all your heart' (Eph. v. 19; cf. Col. iii. 16; James v. 13), refers, as its wording and context make clear, to songs of praise in particular, which of course could include some of the psalms, but could not mean the Psalter as a whole. As the Magnificat of Mary (Luke i. 46–55) and the song of Zachariah (Luke i. 68–73) show, the very first Christians were inspired to produce their own compositions in this field; these poems are little different from those of the Old Testament in form and content; this is also true of the late Jewish imitations of the Psalter (cf. § 13 above). The fragments of early Christian hymns preserved in 1 Tim. iii. 16; Phil. ii. 5–11 and probably also in Rev. v. 9–14 and xix. 1–8 show greater independence. The first definite instances must have been the 'psalms' uttered under direct inspiration, which are mentioned in 1 Cor. xiv. 26.

But notwithstanding the eagerness and delight in singing to the Lord a 'new' song (Rev. v. 9; xiv. 3), we can conclude from the tradition of the Church both in the East and the West that although the Psalter came from the *Old* Testament it soon won for itself a firm place in Christian worship. It was used in different ways: as a scripture reading, as prayer, and to provide hymns for the praise of God. The reading of the Psalter must originally have followed the use of the synagogue, so that it would be followed by a commentary on what had been read; in this case the psalms, like other books of the Old Testament, would bring the word of God to the congregation. The Church also followed the precedent of the synagogue in using the Psalter as a *prayer* book; certain appropriate psalms would be recited at particular moments within an act of worship, and also on particular occasions in the Church year. A later development gave rise to the custom of reciting the *whole Psalter* over a fixed period as a reading or prayer; in the Anglican Church the principle is that this should be done once a month, and in the Roman and Orthodox Churches once a week—during the major fasts of the Eastern Church twice a week. And from the very beginning the Psalter was of the utmost importance as a vehicle for the Church to sing the *praise of God*, although the psalms of praise and thanksgiving were naturally more used for this purpose. By her adherence to the Psalter the Church has continually borne witness to the fact that she belongs to Israel; but by giving the psalms a place in Christian worship, and by concluding them with specific Trinitarian doxologies (e.g., 'Glory be to the Father . . .') it was made quite clear what was intended by this continued use of the psalms.

As for the way in which the psalms were rendered, there already existed in pre-Christian times a solemn melodic chant—the so-called psalmody—besides the usual spoken recitation. Certain psalms were intended from the beginning for 'responsive' use (cf. Pss. xlii–xliii, xlvi, lvii, lxxx and cxxxvi with their recurrent refrains). The 'antiphonal' psalmody, in which the congregation sang or spoke not merely the refrain, but every second verse alternately with the 'cantor' or 'soloist', arose later. The development of more artistic forms of psalmody, and the introduction of the daily prayer of the breviary, resulted in the early Middle Ages in the ever-increasing prominence of clergy and choirs. In so far as the psalms were still sung in worship, and not relegated to the private recitation of the breviary by the clergy, the participation of the congregation was limited to listening to them, and due to the lack, for centuries, of suitable translations, even this was to a large degree impossible for them. It was left to the reformers to rediscover the Psalter for the worshipping community. The very free versions of the psalms by *Luther*, fitted to the tunes of folk-songs, played an essential part in the renewal of the Church, and this is even more true of the 'Huguenot Psalter' which first appeared in its complete version in 1562 at the instigation of *Calvin*. After a catastrophic 'eclipse' during the eighteenth-century Enlightenment this version is still fulfilling the task today—wherever anyone has taken the trouble to make a careful choice and adaptation—of imparting to the Church something of the original power of the psalms.

Something of their original power . . .! For there can be no question of the significance of the Psalter being exhausted in its role as a prayer and hymn book. There is no doubt that it is meant to be frequently read and prayed, recited with devotion, sung and chanted with enthusiasm, always as far as possible by the whole congregation. But the Psalter is intended just as much, if not more, to be *listened* to: as the voice of Israel in harmony with the voice of God and as the voice of God in harmony with the voice of His people. Amongst all the books of the Bible, it is the distinctive quality of the Psalter to bring this harmony to our ears. It is this distinctive note that we have to listen to, and hear in it time and time again 'unheard-of things'.

This listening and new understanding cannot be achieved as long as the Church is content simply to sing and recite the Psalter, and remain content to possess in it a 'revealed' book of prayers and hymns. The idea that it is possible to pray and sing the psalms without serious study is a dangerous illusion. If the message of the psalms is to be heard again, it must be sought out; in the sure expectation, certainly, that it will be heard, but with the honest admission that it is far from being heard at the moment. Throughout the centuries the Church has known how to love the psalms, and to make them loved, for the sake of their profundity, their beauty and their power. As the Church carries on boldly with this task, she must also have the courage to recognise and make clear the whole *strangeness and harshness*, the indelibly 'Israelite' element in the psalms (cf. § 16–19). For this strangeness is not removed, and the very justifiable question as to the 'message' of the psalms is not settled, simply by reciting the Psalter once or twice in

the week—however good and useful a practice that may be
in itself.

This is why the place of the psalms is not merely in the
liturgy, but equally as much in the pulpit, in instruction, and
in 'learned' and 'popular' Bible study groups. The renewal
and reunion of the Church, for which we are hoping, cannot
come about without the powerful assistance of the psalms—
without the support of their incomparable words, and above
all of their imperishable message.

Bibliography

The following works are available in English. The last two listed are more difficult than the others.

The Revised Psalter (the official revision of the Psalter in the Book of Common Prayer in the Church of England (S.P.C.K., 1964)).

A Companion to the Revised Psalter. G. A. Chase (S.P.C.K., 1963).

The Psalms (Layman's Bible Commentaries). A. B. Rhodes (S.C.M. Press, 1961).

The Faith of the Psalmists. H. Ringgren (S.C.M. Press, 1963).

The Psalms and their Meaning for Today. S. Terrien (Bobbs-Merrill, 1952).

The Praise of God in the Psalms. C. Westermann (John Knox Press, 1965).

The Psalms: a Commentary. A. Weiser (S.C.M. Press, 1952).

The Psalms in Israel's Worship. In two volumes. S. Mowinckel (Blackwell, 1962).

Index of Scripture Passages

Other Old Testament Books

Genesis

Exodus

Leviticus

Numbers

Index of Subjects and Authors

84